Helping
Parents
Make Disciples

Helping Parents Make Disciples

Strategic Pastoral Counseling Resources

Everett L. Worthington, Jr.
and Kirby Worthington

Baker Books
A Division of Baker Book House Co
Grand Rapids, Michigan 49516

Published by Baker Books
a division of Baker Book House Company
P.O. Box 6287, Grand Rapids, MI 49516-6287

Printed in the United States of America

Library of Congress Cataloging-in-Publication Data

Worthington, Everett L., 1946–
   Helping parents make disciples : strategic pastoral counseling resources /
Everett L. Worthington, Jr. and Kirby Worthington.
     p. cm.
   Includes bibliographical references.
   ISBN 0-8010-9012-1 (cloth)
   1. Parenting—Religious aspects—Christianity. 2. Child rearing—Religious
aspects—Christianity. 3. Children—Pastoral counseling of, I. Worthington,
Kirby. II. Title.
BV4529.W67 1996
259′.1—dc20   95-37406

To Pat Self,
who has blessed many lives
with her counsel

Contents

Part 4 Examples

post modern
Thought?

An Introduction to Strategic Pastoral Counseling

David G. Benner

While the provision of spiritual counsel has been an integral part of Christian soul care since the earliest days of the church, the contemporary understanding and practice of pastoral counseling is largely a product of the twentieth century. Developing within the shadow of the modern psychotherapies, pastoral counseling has derived much of its style and approach from these clinical therapeutics. What this has meant is that pastoral counselors have often seen themselves more as counselors than as pastors and the counseling that they have provided has often been a rather awkward adaptation of clinical counseling models to a pastoral context. This, in turn, has often resulted in significant tension between the pastoral and psychological dimensions of the counseling provided by clergy and others in Christian ministry. It is also frequently reflected in pastoral counselors who are more interested in anything connected with the modern mystery cult of psychotherapy than with their own tradition of Christian soul care, and who, as a consequence, are often quite insecure in their pastoral role and identity.

While pastoral counseling owes much to the psychological culture which has gained ascendancy in the West during the past century, this influence has quite clearly been a mixed blessing. Contemporary pastoral counselors typically offer their help with much more psychological sophistication than was the case several decades ago, but all too often they do so without a clear sense of the uniqueness of counseling that is offered by a pastor. And not only are the distinctive spiritual resources of Christian ministry often deemphasized or ignored, the tensions that are associated with attempts to directly translate clinical models of counseling into the pastoral context become a source of much frustration. This is in part why so many pastors report dissatisfaction with their counseling. While they indicate that this dissatisfaction is a result of insufficient training in and time for counseling, a bigger part of the problem may be that pastors have been offered approaches to counseling that are of questionable appropriateness for the pastoral context and which will inevitably leave them frustrated and feeling inadequate.

Strategic Pastoral Counseling is a model of counseling which has been specifically designed to fit the role, resources, and needs of the typical pastor who counsels. Information about this "typical" pastor was solicited by means of a survey of over 400 pastors, this research described in the introductory volume of the series, *Strategic Pastoral Counseling: An Overview* (Benner 1992). The model appropriates the insights of contemporary counseling theory without sacrificing the resources of pastoral ministry. Furthermore, it takes its form and direction from the pastoral role and in so doing offers an approach to counseling which is not only congruent with the other aspects of pastoral ministry but which places pastoral counseling at the very heart of ministry.

The present volume represents an application of Strategic Pastoral Counseling to one commonly encountered problem situation. As such, it presupposes a familiarity with the basic model. Readers not familiar with *Strategic Pastoral Counseling: An Overview* should consult this book for a detailed presentation of the model and its implementation. What follows is a brief review of this material which, while it does not adequately summarize all that is presented in that book, should serve as a reminder of the most important features of the Strategic Pastoral Counseling approach.

The Strategic Pastoral Counseling Model

Strategic Pastoral Counseling is short-term, bibliotherapeutic, wholistic, structured, spiritually focused, and explicitly Christian. Each of these characteristics will be briefly discussed in order.

Short-Term Counseling

Counseling can be brief (that is, conducted over a relatively few sessions), or time-limited (that is, conducted within an initially fixed number of total sessions), or both. Strategic Pastoral Counseling is both brief and time-limited, working within a suggested maximum of five sessions. The decision to set this upper limit on the number of sessions was a response to the fact that the background research conducted in the design of the model indicated that 87% of the pastoral counseling conducted by pastors in general ministry involves five sessions or less. This short-term approach to counseling seems ideally suited to the time availability, training, and role demands of pastors.

Recent research in short-term counseling has made clear that while such an approach requires that the counselor be diligent in maintaining the focus on the single agreed-upon central problem, significant and enduring changes can occur through a very small number of counseling sessions. Strategic Pastoral Counseling differs, in this regard, from the more on-going relationship of discipleship or spiritual guidance. In these, the goal is the development of spiritual maturity. Strategic Pastoral Counseling has a much more modest goal, namely, examining a particular problem or experience in the light of God's will for and activity in the life of the individual seeking help and attempting to facilitate that person's growth in and through his or her present life situation. While this is still an ambitious goal, its focused nature makes it quite attainable within a short period of time. It is this focus that makes the counseling strategic.

The five-session limit should be communicated by the pastor no later than the first session and preferably in the prior conversation when the time was set for this session. This ensures that the parishioner is aware of the time limit from the beginning and can share responsibility in keeping the counseling sessions focused. Some people will undoubtedly require more than five sessions in order to bring about a resolution of their problems. These people should be referred to someone who is appropriately qualified for such work and preparation for this referral will be one of the goals of the five sessions. However, the fact that such people may require more than can be provided in five sessions of pastoral counseling does not mean that they cannot benefit from such focused short-term pastoral care and no one should be seen to be inappropriate for Strategic Pastoral Counseling merely because he or she may also require other help.

One final but important note about the suggested limit of five sessions is that this does not have to be tied to a corresponding period of five weeks. In fact, many pastors find weekly sessions to be less useful than sessions scheduled two or three weeks apart. This sort of spacing of the last couple of sessions is particularly helpful and should be considered even if the first several sessions are held weekly.

Bibliotherapeutic Counseling

Bibliotherapy refers to the therapeutic use of reading, and Strategic Pastoral Counseling builds the use of written materials into the heart of its approach to pastoral care giving. The Bible itself is, of course, a rich bibliotherapeutic resource and the encouragement of and direction in its reading is an important part of Strategic Pastoral Counseling. Its use must be disciplined and selective and particular care must be taken to ensure that it is never employed in a mechanical or impersonal manner. However, when used appropriately, it can unquestionably be one of the most dynamic and powerful resources available to the pastor who counsels.

But while the Bible is a unique bibliotherapeutic resource, it is not the only such resource. Strategic Pastoral Counseling comes with a built-in set of specifically designed resources. Each of the ten volumes in this series has an accompanying book written for the parishioner who is being seen in counseling. These resource books are written by the same authors as the volume for pastors and are designed for easy integration into the counseling.

The use of reading materials that are consistent with the counseling being provided can serve as a most significant support and extension of the counseling offered by a pastor. The parishioner now has a helping resource that is not limited by the pastor's time and availability. Furthermore, the pastor can now allow the written materials to do part of the work of counseling, using the sessions to deal with those matters that are not as well addressed through the written page.

Wholistic Counseling

It might seem surprising to suggest that a counseling approach which is short-term should also be wholistic. But this is both possible and highly desirable. Wholistic counseling is counseling which is responsive to the totality of the complex psycho-spiritual dynamics that make up the life of humans. Biblical psychology is clearly a wholistic psychology. The various "parts" of persons (i.e., body, soul, spirit, heart, flesh, etc.) are never presented as separate faculties or independent components of persons but always as different ways of seeing the whole person. Biblical discussions of persons emphasize first and foremost our essential unity of being. Humans are ultimately understandable only in the light of this primary and irreducible wholeness and helping efforts that are truly Christian must resist the temptation to see persons only through their thoughts, feelings, behaviors, or any one other manifestation of being.

The alternative to wholism in counseling is to focus on only one of these modalities of functioning and this is, indeed, what many approaches to counseling do. In contrast to this, Strategic Pastoral Counseling asserts that pastoral counseling must be responsive to the behavioral (action), cognitive (thought), and affective (feeling) elements of personal functioning. Each examined separately can obscure that which is really going on with a person. But taken together they form the basis for a comprehensive assessment and effective intervention. Strategic Pastoral Counseling provides a framework for ensuring that each of these spheres of functioning is addressed and this, in fact, provides much of the structure for counseling.

Structured Counseling

The structured nature of Strategic Pastoral Counseling is that which enables its brevity, the structure ensuring that each of the sessions has a clear focus, and that each builds upon the previous ones in contributing toward the accomplishment of the overall goals. The framework which structures Strategic Pastoral Counseling is sufficiently tight as to enable the pastor to provide a wholistic assessment and counseling intervention within a maximum of five sessions, and yet it is also sufficiently flexible to allow for differences in individual styles of different counselors. This is very important because Strategic Pastoral Counseling is not primarily a set of techniques but is an intimate encounter of and dialogue between two people.

The structure of Strategic Pastoral Counseling grows out of the goal of addressing the feelings, thoughts, and behaviors that are a part of the troubling experiences of the person seeking help. It is also a structure that is responsive to the several tasks that face the pastoral counselor, tasks such as conducting an initial assessment, developing a general understanding of the problem and of the person's major needs, and selecting and delivering interventions and resources that will bring help. This structure is described in more detail later.

Spiritually Focused Counseling

The fourth distinctive of Strategic Pastoral Counseling is that it is spiritually focused. This does not mean that only religious matters are discussed. Our spirituality is our essential heart commitments, our basic life direction, and our fundamental allegiances. These spiritual aspects of our being are, of course, reflected in our attitudes toward God and are expressed in our explicitly religious values and behaviors. However, they are also reflected in matters that may seem on the surface to be much less religious. Strategic Pastoral Counselors place a primacy on listening to this underlying spiritual story. They listen for what we might call the story behind the story.

But listening to the story behind the story requires that one first listen to and take seriously the presenting story. To disregard the presenting situation is spiritualization of a problem. It fails to take the problem seriously and makes a mockery of counseling as genuine dialogue. The Strategic Pastoral Counselor thus listens to and enters into the experience of parishioners as they relate their struggles and life's experiences. But while this is a real part of the story, it is not the whole story that must be heard and understood. For in the midst of this story emerges another, the story of their spiritual response to these experiences. This response may be one of unwavering trust in God but a failure to expect much of Him. Or it may be one of doubt, anger, confusion, or despair. Each of these are spiritual responses to present struggles and, in one form or another, the spiritual aspect of the person's experience will always be discernible to the pastor who watches for it. The Strategic Pastoral Counselor makes this underlying spiritual story the primary focus.

Explicitly Christian Counseling

But while it is important to not confuse spirituality with religiosity, it is equally important to not confuse Christian spirituality with any of its imitations. In this regard, it is crucial that Strategic Pastoral Counseling begins with a focus on spiritual matters understood broadly; its master goal is to facilitate the other person's awareness of and response to the call of God to surrender and service. This is the essential and most important distinctive of Strategic Pastoral Counseling.

One of the ways in which Strategic Pastoral Counseling is made explicitly Christian is through its utilization of Christian theological language, images, and concepts, and the religious resources of prayer, scriptures, and the sacraments. As pointed out earlier, these resources must never be used in a mechanical, legalistic, or magical fashion. But used sensitively and wisely, they can be the conduit for a dynamic contact between God and the person seeking pastoral help. And this is the goal of their utilization, not some superficial baptizing of the counseling in order to make it Christian but rather a way of bringing the one seeking help more closely in touch with the God who is the source of all life, growth, and healing.

Another important resource that is appropriated by the Strategic Pastoral Counselor is that of the church as a community. Too often pastoral counseling is conducted in a way that is not appreciably different from that which might be offered by a Christian counselor in private practice. This most unfortunate practice ignores the rich resources that are potentially available in any Christian congregation. One of the most important ways in which Strategic Pastoral Counseling is able to maintain its short-term nature is by the pastor connecting the person seeking help with others in the church who can provide portions of that help. The congregation can, of course, also be involved in less individualistic ways. Support and ministry groups of various sorts are becoming a part of many congregations that seek to provide a dynamic ministry to their community and are potentially most important resources for the Strategic Pastoral Counselor.

A final and even more fundamental way in which Strategic Pastoral Counseling is Christian is in the reliance that it encourages on the Holy Spirit. The Spirit is the indispensable source of all wisdom that is necessary for the practice of pastoral counseling. Recognizing that all healing and growth is ultimately of God, the Strategic Pastoral Counselor can thus take comfort in this reliance on the Spirit of God and on the fact that ultimate responsibility for the person and his or her well-being lies with God.

Stages and Tasks of Strategic Pastoral Counseling

The three overall stages which organize Strategic Pastoral Counseling can be described as Encounter, Engagement, and Disengagement. The first stage of Strategic Pastoral Counseling, Encounter, corresponds to the initial session where the goal is to establish a personal contact with the person seeking help, set the boundaries for the counseling relationship, become acquainted with the person and his or her central concerns, conduct a pastoral diagnosis, and develop a mutually acceptable focus for the subsequent sessions. The second stage, Engagement, involves the pastor moving beyond the first contact and establishing a deeper working alliance with the person seeking help. This normally occupies the next one to three sessions and entails the exploration of the person's feelings, thoughts, and behavioral patterns associated with this problem area and the development of new perspectives and strategies for coping or change. The third and final stage, Disengagement, describes the focus of the last one or possibly two sessions which involve an evaluation of progress and an assessment of remaining concerns, the making of a referral for further help if this is needed, and the ending of the counseling relationship. These stages and tasks are summarized in Table 1.

Stages and Tasks of Strategic Pastoral Counseling

Stage 1:   Encounter (Session 1)
* Joining and boundary-setting
* Exploring the central concerns and relevant history
* Conducting a pastoral diagnosis
* Achieving a mutually agreeable focus for counseling

Stage 2:   Engagement (Sessions 2, 3, 4)
* Exploration of cognitive, affective, and behavioral aspects of the problem and the identification of resources for coping or change

Stage 3:   Disengagement (Session 5)
* Evaluation of progress and assessment of remaining concerns
* Referral (if needed)
* Termination of counseling

The Encounter Stage

The first task in this initial stage of Strategic Pastoral Counseling is joining and boundary setting. Joining involves putting the parishioner at ease by means of a few moments of casual conversation that is designed to ease pastor and parishioner into contact. Such preliminary conversation should never take more than five minutes and should usually be kept to two or three. And not always will it be necessary, some people being immediately ready to tell their story. Boundary setting involves the communication of the purpose of this session and the time frame for the session, and your work together. This should not normally require more than a sentence or two.

The exploration of central concerns and relevant history usually begins with an invitation for the parishioner to describe what led him or her to seek help at the present time. After hearing an expression of these immediate concerns, it is usually helpful to get a brief historical perspective on these concerns and the person. Ten to fifteen minutes of exploration of the course of development of the presenting problems and efforts to cope or get help with them is the foundation of this part of the session. It is also important at this point to get some idea of the parishioner's present living and family arrangements as well as his or her work or educational situation. The organizing thread for this section of the first interview should be the presenting problem. These matters will not be the only ones discussed, but this focus serves to give the session the necessary direction.

Stripped of its distracting medical connotations, diagnosis is problem definition, and this is a fundamental part of any approach to counseling. Diagnoses involve judgments about the nature of the problem and, either implicitly or explicitly, pastoral counselors make such judgments every time they commence a counseling relationship. But in order for diagnoses to be relevant, they must guide the counseling which will follow. This means that the categories of pastoral assessment must be primarily related to the spiritual focus which is foundational to any counseling that is appropriately called pastoral. Thus, the diagnosis which is called for in the first stage of Strategic Pastoral Counseling involves an assessment of the person's spiritual well-being.

The framework for pastoral diagnosis adopted by Strategic Pastoral Counseling is that suggested by Malony (1988) and used as the basis of his *Religious Status Interview*. Malony proposed that the diagnosis of Christian religious well-being should involve the assessment of the person's awareness of God, acceptance of God's grace, repentance and responsibility, response to God's leadership and direction, involvement in the church, experience of fellowship, ethics, and openness in faith. While this approach to pastoral diagnosis has been found to be helpful by many, the Strategic Pastoral Counselor need not feel confined by it. It is offered as a suggested framework for conducting a pastoral assessment, and each individual pastoral counselor needs to approach this task in ways that fit his or her own theological convictions and personal style. Further details on the conduct of a pastoral assessment can be found in *Strategic Pastoral Counseling: An Overview* (Benner 1992).

The final task of the Encounter stage of Strategic Pastoral Counseling is achieving a mutually agreeable focus for counseling. Often this is self-evident, made immediately clear by the first expression of the parishioner. At other times, parishioners will report a wide range of concerns in the first session and will have to be asked what should constitute the primary problem focus. The identification of the primary problem focus leads naturally to a formulation of goals for the counseling. These goals will sometimes be quite specific (i.e., to be able to make an informed decision about a potential job change) but will also at times be rather broad (i.e., to be able to express feelings related to an illness). As is illustrated in these examples, some goals will describe an end point while others will describe more of a process. Maintaining this flexibility in how goals are understood is crucial if Strategic Pastoral Counseling is to be a helpful counseling approach for the broad range of situations faced by the pastoral counselor.

The Engagement Stage

The second stage of Strategic Pastoral Counseling involves the further engagement of pastor and the one seeking help around the problems and concerns that brought them together. This is the heart of the counseling process. The major tasks of this stage are the exploration of the person's feelings, thoughts, and behavioral patterns associated with the central concerns, and the development of new perspectives and strategies for coping or change.

It is important to note that the work of this stage may well begin in the first session. The model should not be interpreted in a rigid or mechanical manner. If the goals of the first stage are completed with time remaining in the first session, one can very appropriately begin to move into the tasks of this next stage. However, once the tasks of Stage 1 are completed, those associated with this second stage become the central focus. If the full five sessions of Strategic Pastoral Counseling are employed, this second stage normally provides the structure for sessions 2, 3, and 4.

The central focus for the three sessions normally associated with this stage are, respectively, the feelings, thoughts, and behaviors associated with the problem presented by the person seeking help. Although these are usually intertwined, a selective focus on each, one at a time, ensures that each is adequately addressed and that all the crucial dynamics of the person's psychospiritual functioning are considered.

The reason for beginning with feelings is that this is where most people themselves begin when they come to a counselor. But this does not mean that most people know their feelings. The exploration of feelings involves encouraging the person to face and express whatever it is that they are feeling, to the end that these feelings can be known and then dealt with appropriately. The goal at this point is to listen and respond empathically to the feelings of the one seeking help, not to try to change them.

After an exploration of the major feelings being experienced by the person seeking help, the next task is an exploration of the thoughts associated with these feelings and the development of alternative ways of understanding present experiences. It is in this phase of Strategic Pastoral Counseling that the explicit use of scriptures is usually most appropriate. Bearing in mind the potential misuses and problems that can be associated with such use of religious resources, the pastoral counselor should be, nonetheless, open to a direct presentation of scriptural truths when they offer the possibility of a new and helpful perspective on one's situation.

The final task of the Engagement stage of Strategic Pastoral Counseling grows directly out of this work on understanding and involves the exploration of the behavioral components of the person's functioning. Here the pastor explores what concrete things the person is doing in the face of the problems or distressing situations being encountered and together with the parishioner begins to identify changes in behavior that may be desirable. The goal of this stage is to identify changes that both pastor and parishioner agree are important and to begin to establish concrete strategies for making these changes.

The Disengagement Stage

The last session or two involves preparation for the termination of counseling and includes two specific tasks, the evaluation of progress and assessment of remaining concerns and making arrangements regarding a referral if this is needed.

The evaluation of progress is usually a process that both pastor and parishioner will find to be rewarding. Some of this may be done during previous sessions. But even when this is the case, it is a good idea to use the last session to undertake a brief review of what has been learned from the counseling. Closely associated with this, of course, is an identification of remaining concerns. Seldom is everything resolved after 5 sessions. This means that the parishioner is preparing to leave counseling with some work yet to be done. But he or she does so with plans for the future and the development of these is an important task of the Disengagement stage of Strategic Pastoral Counseling.

If significant problems remain at this point, the last couple of sessions should also be used to make referral arrangements. Ideally these should be discussed in the second or third session and they should by now be all arranged. It might even be ideal if by this point the parishioner should have had a first session with the person whom he or she will be seeing, thus allowing a processing of this first experience as part of the final pastoral counseling session.

Recognition of one's own limitations of time, experience, training, and ability is an indispensable component of the practice of all professionals. Pastors are no exceptions. Pastors offering Strategic Pastoral Counseling need, therefore, to be aware of the resources within their community and to be prepared to refer parishioners for help that they can better receive elsewhere.

In the vast majority of cases, the actual termination of a Strategic Pastoral Counseling relationship goes very smoothly. Most often, both pastor and parishioner agree that there is not further need to meet, and they find easy agreement with, even if some sadness around, the decision to discontinue the counseling sessions. However, there may be times when this process is somewhat difficult. This will sometimes be due to the parishioner's desire to continue to meet. At other times, the difficulty in terminating will reside within the pastor. Regardless, the best course of action is usually to follow through on the initial limits agreed upon by both parties.

The exception to this rule is a situation where the parishioner is facing some significant stress or crisis at the end of the five sessions and where there are no other available resources to provide the support that he or she needs. If this is the situation, an extension of a few sessions may be appropriate. However, this should again be time-limited and should take the form of crisis management. It should not involve more sessions than is absolutely necessary to restore some degree of stability to the parishioner's functioning or to introduce them to other people who can be of assistance.

Conclusion

Strategic Pastoral Counseling provides a framework for pastors who seek to counsel in a way that is congruent with the rest of their pastoral responsibilities and which is psychologically informed and responsible. While skill in implementing the model comes only over time, because the approach is focused and time-limited, it is quite possible for most pastors to acquire these skills. However, counseling skills cannot be adequately learned simply by reading books. As with all interpersonal skills, they must be learned through practice, and ideally, this practice is best acquired in a context of supervisory feedback from a more experienced pastoral counselor.

The pastor who has mastered the skills of Strategic Pastoral Counseling is in a position to proclaim the Word of God in a highly personalized and relevant manner to people who are often desperate for help. This is a unique and richly rewarding opportunity. Rather than scattering seed in a broadcast manner across ground that is often stony and hard even if at places it is also fertile and receptive to growth, the pastoral counselor has the opportunity to carefully plant one seed at a time. Knowing the soil conditions, he or she is also able to plant it in a highly individualized manner, taking pains to ensure that it will not be quickly blown away, and then gently watering and nourishing its growth. This is the unique opportunity for the ministry of Strategic Pastoral Counseling. It is my prayer that pastors will see the centrality of counseling to their call to ministry, feel encouraged by the presence of an approach to pastoral counseling that lies within their skills and time availability, and will take up these responsibilities with renewed vigor and clarity of direction.

References

Benner, D. G. (1992). *Strategic pastoral counseling: An overview.* Grand Rapids, Mich.: Baker Book House.

Malony, H. N. (1988). "The clinical assessment of optimal religious functioning." *Review of Religious Research,* 30(1), 3–17.

Preface

Parents and pastors have a lot in common. Both are on call day and night, rarely have a day off, are expected to know all the answers (parents and pastors are both perfect, aren't they?), and feel pressure to feed their sheep. Pastors and parents serve, at times, as prophets, priests, and leaders of our domains, so that those in our care can learn personally of God. The tasks of pastor and parent are similar: disciple those less mature, intercede as a peacemaker in conflicts, help restore to fellowship the repentant sinner, periodically give sermons (though these are less well-received from parents), and organize and lead in a godly direction. Both pastor and parent feel (1) lack of control when we do our best and those in our care want to go elsewhere and act on different values than we espouse, (2) hurt when those in our care grumble, complain, criticize, and reject our leadership, and (3) joy when we see those in our care act in faith and love.

The secret of being a good parent or pastor (or Christian in general) is the same: produce disciples of Christ from those around you by practicing "faith working through love" (Gal. 5:6). This book shows you, who are called by God to be a pastor-counselor, how to help parents make disciples of their children. At the same time, you'll be answering your high calling as pastor by helping parents become better disciples of Christ. We pray that, through reading this book, you, your parishioners, and their children will benefit and the kingdom of God will be strengthened.

Part 1

Fundamentals

1

Why Strategic Pastoral Counseling for Parents?

All I ever needed to know about parenting, I learned before my kids were in kindergarten," said one pastor, tongue slightly in cheek, when he found that we were writing about parenting.

In this book, we tell you three primary things. We provide:

- a pastoral view of parenting as making disciples through applying a single vital Christian principle,
- a three-stage, five-session method to teach the principle during counseling, and
- examples of how to apply the principle with several common parenting problems.

Introduction to Counseling Families

The first family I counseled started as an individual client.[1] After church one Sunday, a 25-year-old college student had lost his temper and hit his wife on the arm. She said he had a problem, so he

1. I tell this story in more detail in Worthington (1992).

showed up at the Counseling Center and avowed on the intake form that his problem was "GROSS CHARACTER DEFECT"—a diagnosis perhaps suggested by his wife. I proposed that he follow a tried-and-true treatment for controlling his anger. "It'll take only seven sessions," I said.

He looked like I had pole-axed him between the eyes with a two-by-four. "I didn't think it would take so long," he said.

I confess that to me seven sessions to help with a GROSS CHARACTER DEFECT seemed to border on optimism. He agreed, reluctantly, to the seven-week cure, and it soon became apparent that he and his wife were having marital problems. He lost his temper in arguments with his wife. So, in she came, complete with seven-month-old Joey glued to her hip. Ah, family counseling. I had read about it. It seemed straightforward when the masters did it. How hard could it be?

While I worked with the parents on their marital conflicts, Joey rearranged all the books on my bookshelf, ate a small potted plant, systematically pulled every tissue from the box, turned over my (unplugged, thank the Lord) coffee pot, and ate things he found in my carpet. When he tired of that, he crawled over and chinned himself on my inner thigh. (Almost twenty years later, the hair is growing back.)

I interrupted one particularly loud argument between the parents and suggested that they were in a power struggle. They wheeled toward me in unison, veins bulging in their necks, and together said, "We are *not* in a power struggle. We are merely *discussing the issues*." (Counselor, stunned, swallows bubble gum.) They then resumed "discussing the issues." Loudly.

Fortunately, since I recorded sessions, the interaction was preserved on audiotape. When my supervisor listened to the session, she noticed that the "discussion of the issues" had provoked the child to tears. The next week, I replayed the tape for the couple, who were then convinced to work on their marriage, which seemed to be connected to the child's crying and to the husband's anger.

After twelve weeks we had made substantial progress. The husband's anger was under control (GROSS CHARACTER DEFECT apparently in remission), the parents argued more constructively (and softly), and Joey was more eventempered. Everyone was pleased. Joey was so happy he left me a pile of slobber-soaked Cheerios on my chair, which I later sat on and wore for the remainder of the day.

One small dark cloud appeared on the horizon. As we ended counseling, the wife thanked me and asked for the name of a female therapist that she could consult about her depression. Symptom substitution within the family had reared its ugly head.

After reflecting on the case for weeks, I got over my own depression (due to symptom substitution, not wet Cheerios). I concluded that despite the wife's depression, we had helped the husband control his anger and the parents manage their conflict better and work more effectively with their child.

I was no longer cocky about family therapy, especially in the hands of a novice such as myself. I had found that family counseling is confusing. With each additional participant, I learned more, saw more sides of the problem, and gained perspective; paradoxically, I lost focus. Were my goals to help the husband, the wife, the marriage, the parents, the family, Joey? I staggered about like a drunken sailor, moving from goal to goal, crisis to crisis. I didn't have a strategy. Counseling was a shotgun blast. I aimed counseling in a general direction and hoped to hit something vital. I was enamored with techniques of counseling, and I used them to deal with momentary crises. I needed a rifle with a telescopic sight.

In this book, we hope to arm you with a rifle-like strategy to target vital parenting problems. We will show you how to build parents' faith and provide you with the confidence to pull the trigger to counsel effectively.

Be Clear about Who Your Counselee Is and What Your Goals Are

One reason counseling for parenting problems can stray is because parents usually present their problems by saying, "How do I help my child who is having problems with . . . ?" At first blush, the problem sounds as if it is the child's problem. Over the years, though, counselors have found that counseling usually isn't effective if the counselor tries to help a person who isn't coming to counseling—in this case, the child.

Think of the problem as the parents', but in a constructive, not blaming, way. Help parents understand that they cannot change their child. Parents can only help their child by changing themselves. You will generally have three goals:

- To arm parents with a strategy for helping the child handle the problem while building the child's faith, thus making the child a better disciple of Christ.
- To bolster the parents' self-confidence to parent through building their Christian discipleship, providing information, helping develop (or improve) parenting skills, and sensitizing them to notice their successes and correct their failures.
- To connect the parents to a supportive healing community.

Inherent in our approach is pastoral counseling's major objective: to make stronger disciples of Jesus Christ through working to solve parents' problems in dealing with their children. A disciple of Jesus has accepted Christ as Savior and Lord and is motivated by love and gratitude to follow Jesus with discipline, living (through faith) a pattern of love and work described throughout Scripture. If Strategic Pastoral Counseling works well, both the parents and children should become more faithful disciples of Jesus and should have fewer problems.

Do Parents Consult Pastors for Parenting Problems?

In preparing for this series in Strategic Pastoral Counseling, Baker Book House surveyed 405 pastors in the United States and Canada (Benner 1992). Each pastor was asked to name what he or she thought to be the five most common problems seen in pastoral counseling. Thirty-one percent named problems with children as one of the five. Seven problems were mentioned more frequently: marriage (84 percent), depression (64 percent), addictions (44 percent), guilt (38 percent), grief (37 percent), unforgiveness (37 percent), and worry or anxiety (33 percent). Eight problems were mentioned less frequently. Consider this: Much marital disharmony involves conflict over how the partners parent, depression may occur when parents can't control their children, parents worry about their children, and much inferiority, guilt, and child abuse occur because people feel out-of-control in parenting. The average pastor will probably counsel many parents. Counseling parents effectively is thus a substantial ministry.

It's Simple

Simple Solutions

Every approach to parenting that has been widely accepted over the last half century has been fundamentally simple. Of course, in hindsight, we can see some mistakes in each method, but our point is not to analyze those mistakes as much as to observe the simplicity in each approach.

For instance, Benjamin Spock (1945) advocated permissive parenting. Parents were admonished to use the child's behavior as their guideline for how to parent. Children were assumed to be basically good, and parents were seen as squelching the goodness through harsh, punitive training. Many of a generation of children, baby-boomers, were reared by parents who practiced some variation of Spock's approach. In 1968, at the Democratic National Convention in Chicago, a nation of parents saw via live television the result of permissive parenting—the clash of rebelliousness and authoritarian repression.

For many, the theories of Maria Montessori (1964, 1972) were attractive. Montessori believed that children hungered for learning. Parents could promote learning through presenting an exciting learning environment with a structure that channeled children's energy into learning and didn't use a permissive approach. Montessori's approach was given credence by the increasingly popular theory of mental development proposed by Swiss biologist and psychologist Jean Piaget (1959), who also assumed that children wanted to learn and would do so naturally if placed in enriched environments.

More politically and socially moderate parents were drawn to programs like Thomas Gordon's (1975) Parent Effectiveness Training (PET). Based on the theory of Carl Rogers (1951), which also assumed that children were basically good, PET emphasized listening to children, understanding their worldview, and using adult reasoning to guide children to obtain their goals. Parent-child negotiation became the way to good parenting according to PET.

Many Christians focused on parenting approaches that emphasized parental authority. Parental authority was to be enforced by firm rules, consistent discipline, nurturant love, and family closeness. Proponents of such approaches were James Dobson (*Dare To Discipline*, 1970; *Love Must Be Tough*, 1983), Bill Gothard (*Institute in Basic Youth Conflicts*, 1981), and Larry Christenson (*The Christian Family*, 1970). These approaches assumed that children are naturally self-centered and must be trained to be loving. These approaches are called "authoritative" parenting.

The effects on children of permissive and authoritative approaches to child rearing have been studied. Diana Baumrind (1967, 1971) found that authoritative parenting produced the most self-reliant, self-controlled, content, friendly, cooperative, and high-achieving children. Other research (see Berger 1988 for a summary) has found that children raised by authoritative parenting are more successful, happy with themselves, and generous with others; whereas, children raised by permissive parenting were less self-controlled and self-reliant and more unhappy. Sons of permissive parents were found to be particularly low achieving.

Simple Strategy, Not So Simple to Put into Action

In each case, the solution to parenting difficulties has been relatively simple—provide support without punishing (Spock), provide learning-rich environments (Montessori), teach negotiation (Gordon), help parents be firmly controlling and nurturant (Dobson). However, putting these solutions into action during daily trials and larger crises that confront parents has not been simple to do. Parenting engages a jumble of emotions, thoughts, and behaviors, including love, concern for our children, worry about how others will perceive us as parents, elation over our child's successes, deflation over our child's failures, control issues, our own level of stress, our own problems, our relationships with our mate, and even our relationships with our own parents. On top of this symphony of reactions, the sheer weight of habit forces us into familiar patterns of behavior that we may have learned in our own childhood and may perform without a second thought.

Without a simple strategy—one that a parent can bear constantly in mind and repeat throughout the day—parenting will be kneejerk thoughtless reactions that will not contribute to the furthering of the kingdom of God. This is why God commanded the Israelites,

> Hear, O Israel: The LORD our God is one LORD; and you shall love the LORD your God with all your heart, and with all your soul, and with all your might. And these words which I command you this day shall be upon your heart; and you shall teach them diligently to your children, and shall talk of them when you sit in your house, and when you walk by the way, and when you lie down, and when you rise. And you shall bind them as a sign upon your hand, and they shall be as frontlets between your eyes. And you shall write them on the doorposts of your house and on your gates (Deut. 6:4–9).

God commands Israel to (1) have faith in God, (2) love God, and (3) work hard to teach and show a reflection of this love to children and others. If we want to follow God's plan for parenting—indeed for disciplined Christian living—we must adhere to the simple, yet hard-to-do strategy laid out in the beginning: faith working through love. You can teach this strategy to your parishioners, who teach it to their children. God calls each of us to witness to others, who in turn witness to their spiritual children. Thus, Strategic Pastoral Counseling for parents is rooted in God's basic message to his creatures: live by faith working through love.

2

The Challenge of Parenting in the Twenty-First Century

C hange inevitably makes us follow new routes to reach our destinations.

When we moved to Richmond sixteen years ago, we lived just inside the outer perimeter of the metropolitan Richmond area. Today we live in that same house, but it seems to be the center of a twelve-mile shopping center amid fast food restaurants, grocery stores, gas stations, and apartment complexes. It's hard to find our way around our old neighborhood, and traveling across town is like learning a maze.

Like negotiating city streets, helping parents isn't like it used to be. Your goal—promoting mature disciples of Jesus Christ—is the same despite the changes in society and in families, but the routes to this goal are different. Gone are the days when you could expect that the only people coming to you with parenting problems were members of two-parent families. Many families are different today, and so is the world in which families exist.

Twenty-First-Century Families

The traditional family is under pressure. While death of a spouse has broken families at a relatively constant rate over the recent decades, divorce has assaulted the family. Divorce rates are at an all-time high (Glenn 1989), resulting in two prevalent alternatives to the traditional nuclear family.

- Remarried families. Some people estimate, based on U.S. Census Bureau statistics, that currently one of five children is a step-child, that up to a third of all children born in the 1980s will live with a step-parent before they are eighteen, and that by the year 2000 step-families will outnumber both intact nuclear families and single-parent households (Visher & Visher 1988).
- Single-parent families. The number of children living in households headed by a single mother has increased from five million in 1960 to fourteen million in 1990 (U.S. Census Bureau, annual). About two million additional children live in a household headed by a single father.

Other living arrangements exist, such as child-rearing households headed by homosexual couples, cohabiting couples, and artificially inseminated women. With this array of family forms, it seems that traditional two-parent headed families are scarce. Not true. Of all United States children, 58 percent are reared in two-parent households with both biological parents and 14 percent are reared in families headed by two step-parents. Twenty-two percent of the children are reared in mother-child families, three percent in father-child families, and three percent in other arrangements (such as grandparents, institutional housing, and foster care) (Family Research Council 1992).

For you, the pastor, this implies that you can't assume that only couples will have parenting problems. You'll frequently encounter working mothers who are struggling to rear children amid enormous economic, home-maintenance, and child-rearing pressures. Step-families are common and most step-families are more stressful than are traditional nuclear families.

Understanding the Effects
of Modern Pressures on the Family

To many, life seems to be a roller coaster run amok on tracks that extend into a hidden future. Loss of control is the primary effect of the rapid changes that have characterized life in the late twentieth-century United States. That loss of control shows up in several arenas.

Loss of Control over Time

Time has become a tyrant whose name is Now. People don't want to wait for gratification; they want it now. We have moved from mechanical to electronic technology, so everything happens faster than it used to.

One institution affected the most by the time crunch has been the family. Time spent with children has dramatically atrophied in recent years (Nock & Kingston 1988; Robinson 1977, 1989). While time has crunched all parents, it has dealt especially harshly with two-earner families. Steve Nock and Paul William Kingston found that employed mothers spent less than half as much time with their preschool children as did nonemployed homemaker mothers. Further, "high-quality," child-centered interactions were also only half as frequent with employed mothers as with nonemployed mothers. Nock and Kingston also found that fathers in dual-earner families spent less time with their children than parents in single-earner families. Feelings of parental guilt result (Family Research Council 1992).

As pastor, don't merely exhort parents to spend more time with their children. Parents *want* to spend more time, but they can't seem to make themselves do it. Rather than exhortation and additional guilt, parents need understanding, compassion, workable strategies for *how* they can spend more time with their children, and help at accomplishing the goals they have for themselves and their children.

Loss of Control to Other Caretakers

Who is controlling the children if parents don't have the time? A myriad of caretakers, including day-care workers, teachers, and electronic baby-sitters (such as television, rental videotapes, and videogames). These parental surrogates aren't doing well at tending the children. Day care can work well if qualified workers are found, but many workers aren't qualified and low wages keep many qualified workers moving toward higher-paying jobs. Recently, schools have come under great criticism, and parents have long been dissatisfied with media.

Loss of Control over the Ability to Cope with Stress

Most parents feel that they are under great stress. Stress has many predictable negative effects.

Stress makes parents more egocentric. When stress rises, adults are troubled and think about their own troubles. Focusing on one's pain and trouble is a natural reaction, designed to help solve the problems and avoid danger. However, children can be virtually ignored when parental stress is high. With high work demands and with the current idea that children deserve special experiences (sports teams, dance lessons, and the like), even after-work hours often must be as precisely scheduled as a European train system to keep a household functioning. Human error, unexpected meetings, car failure, or any unscheduled activity can disrupt schedules and create frustration, anger, and more stress.

Stress lowers the threshold for defining a behavior as being a problem. Rex Forehand and his colleagues from the University of Georgia have suggested that parents tolerate "normal misbehavior" (Forehand, Wells, McMahon, Griest, & Rogers 1982). At some point, though, parents may define misbehavior as being a "problem" and seek help from a pastor or mental health professional. High stress lowers the threshold for defining a behavior as abnormal. Many parents under stress who seek counseling because the child won't obey actually have better-behaved children than do parents not under stress.

Stress results in psychological and physical problems. Researchers have documented a wide array of stress-related disorders. Depression, anxiety, alcoholism, and other psychological problems are intensified when a person is under stress. Physical problems, too, like cancer, heart and cardiovascular problems, and gastrointestinal problems (colitis, ulcers, spastic colon) may be affected by stress. If parents develop psychological or physical problems, other family members usually feel burdened. Parenting can be seriously affected if one parent is dealing with a chronic problem and the other parent is occupied taking care of that spouse.

Loss of Control over Social Support

Parents under stress often have little time to devote to friends and extended family members, who are often under stress of their own. Thus, during the child-rearing years, many parents' social-support networks are depleted. Parents are often so stressed that they can't support each other as marital partners. Marital satisfaction decreases with the birth of a child and with the birth of each successive child (Olson et al. 1983). Much of this decrease is due to the extra duties that must be done once a person becomes a parent. Demands suck up the time needed for good marital relations.

Implications of Dealing with Twenty-First-Century Parents

Understand Parents and Their Children

Needs. People have one central need: to discover meaning in life. They attempt to meet this need as they strive to meet two related needs for (1) *effectance*, which is the sense that a person can produce meaningful effects in life (through work, relationships, or leisure), and (2) *intimacy* in relationships (with God and other people they value and feel valued by). These needs have been recognized from antiquity. In the Garden of Eden God created Adam for effectance: to have dominion over the animals (Gen. 1:26) and to work in the Garden (Gen. 2:15). He created Eve (Gen. 2:18) to help Adam work and to fulfill his need for a mate. Children and adults meet their needs for effectance and intimacy in many ways. Children need reasonable moral guidelines to provide a sense of effectance. They also need to experience a sense of God's holiness and steadfastness. Children obtain a sense of intimacy when they know that they are loved, valued, and understood. They feel intimate with God by appropriating God's love, acceptance, and forgiveness. Parents obtain a sense of effectance through interactions with their mate and through affecting their children. A sense of intimacy is obtained through close interactions with the mate, but also through loving and valuing the children and being loved and valued by them.

Threats to parents' needs. When parents and children do not feel understood by each other, their fundamental needs are threatened. They don't feel that they can have the effects on each other that they would like, nor do they feel as valued, loved, and accepted by each other as they would like.

Pastor's response. Make understanding a primary goal of counseling. Begin by understanding each participant. Understand the mother's perspective on the problem and show that you understand her and value her point of view. Understand the father's perspective, which may differ from the mother's, and convey to the father—if he is present in counseling—that you understand him. Finally, try to understand the child's perspective. How is the child being threatened? Why isn't the child feeling effective and intimate? How can the child be helped to feel more effective and intimate?

Parents won't listen to your counsel unless they believe that you understand them. Most parents with problem children say that professionals do not understand their problems, children, and frustrations (Strommen & Strommen 1985). Make understanding a main aim.

Help Parents Regain a Sense of Control

Don't simply take over. Pressures undermine parents' sense of control in many areas (time, caretakers, stress, and social support). When children are having problems serious enough for the parents to seek your help, the normal feelings of loss of control are magnified by not being able to help their child. Help the parents regain a sense of control. If you simply step in and solve the child's and parents' problem, you *take away* parental control, not help restore it.

Support parents in doing their job. Affirm at the beginning that parents will, must, and should raise their children. Pastors encourage and support them and provide help with problems. In 1 Thessalonians 5:14, Paul says Christians are to "encourage the timid, help the weak, be patient with everyone." Parents need special encouragement.

Help break the negative control cycle. Help parents regain a sense of control by smashing negative uncontrollable cycles of behavior between children and parents. When a child misbehaves, parents feel control slipping away, and they may try to restore their control by overpowering the child—forcing obedience on the child. Many times, such as when the child is in danger or directly disobedient, love requires correction, training, and punishment, but these times should be infrequent. Frequent negative control constricts the child, who may break out by misbehaving. This is especially true in the teen years. Parents feel less in control and try harsher restrictions. The cycle can grow until an explosion occurs.

To break the negative-control cycle requires faith working through love. Faith says that love will conquer power. Faith is required that parents can value their children and restore a sense of control to the child (and to themselves), and the active love will have a stronger effect than overcoming power with power. Love is valuing, and not devaluing, the child. Work, too, is required. Work is the constant application of the principle of faith working through love.

Help parents deal with time pressures. Most parents say they don't have the time and energy to deal effectively with problems. The bad news: work is necessary. The good news: it's easier to work in a positive environment than in a negative, conflictual, angry environment. Work is needed regardless of whether parents exert effort positively or whether they allow problems to worsen. In the long run it takes far less energy to act effectively early than to deal with years of pain produced by parental inaction.

When the child begins to behave, the incentive wanes for parents to continue to work on their parenting. Help them keep working on their parenting. Most come looking for a simple command, a motivational tool, an easy-to-apply method of returning the child to harmony and relieving the stress of dealing with the child's problems. They are looking for the perfect method of discipline, the flawless technique, the easy way out. There is no quick fix. Love requires work and time. Knowing this, you can act appropriately as a motivator and encourager rather than as the savior parents want you to be.

Lower Guilt, Don't Increase It

Most parents feel guilty, inferior, and inadequate—especially if their child is having problems. They feel like failures as parents. Instead of heaping guilt on parents by dwelling on their failures, support them and build their confidence that God chose them to parent and will equip them to parent. Past failures are no cause to be depressed. They are a spur to change.

Summary

Parenting in modern times is challenging. Help point parents back to their relationship with Jesus and the Scriptures, which provide a sense of stability, values, hope, power, and love. Restore a sense of control to parents by conveying a godly understanding of the causes of their parenting difficulties—an understanding that will lead them into closer relationships with each other and with God. (See Table 2–1 for a summary.)

TABLE 2–1
The Pastor's Role in Changing
Family Problems into Family Solutions

Difficulties Meeting This Need Meaning	Produce Problems in These Areas	Pastor Tries to Promote Hope	Produces Renewed Sense of Meaning
Effectance	Faith Work	Motivation to Try	Effectance
Intimacy	Love	Willingness to Value	Intimacy

3

The Root Cause
of Parenting Problems

Marita, sixteen, had come home at 2:00 A.M. again. Mary Rae
rose from her bed and walked to the door of the living room. She
stood in the doorway, leaning cross-armed against the door jamb,
as Marita stumbled toward the bedroom, oblivious to Mary Rae's
presence. Marita dropped one shoe and bent to retrieve it. Losing
her balance, she staggered into the lamp, knocking it to the floor.
She put her finger to her lips, "Ssshhh," she indicated to the lamp.

"You're drunk," said Mary Rae.

Marita dropped the other shoe and looked blearily at her mother.
"Yeah, right," she said sarcastically.

"And you're late. You come home two hours after your curfew
so drunk or stoned that you can't even stand up and . . ."

"Ah, stuff it," said Marita. She kicked her shoe across the room
and walked past Mary Rae toward her bedroom.

Mary Rae followed, gushing a stream of criticism.

Marita raised her arm and flapped her fingers toward her thumb
in a talking motion. "Blah, blah, blah," she said. She jerked back
the covers of her bed and fell face down.

Mary Rae was livid. She screamed, "You're nothing but a young tramp. You're no good. You're . . ." She reached down and grabbed Marita's arm jerking her onto her side. "You're . . ."

Marita emitted a small snore.

Mary Rae was furious, but she recognized that nothing would be accomplished in a discussion tonight. She pushed Marita onto her side and stormed from the room.

In her own bedroom, Mary Rae began to plan her intended next morning's discussion with Marita. This wasn't the first time that Marita had come home late and drunk, but Mary Rae was determined that it would be the last—if she had anything to do with it. She was finished with the rebellious child. *Let her father deal with her*, Mary Rae thought. She didn't relish calling Johnnie and having him drive from Massachusetts to take custody of Marita, but Mary Rae also refused to continue to fight with Marita while her ex-husband lived a carefree bachelor life. She paced the bedroom, knowing that it would be hours before her adrenaline decreased. Her mind raced through an imaginary conversation with Johnnie. Exhausted, she couldn't sleep.

Parenting as Discipleship

God has a pattern for life within the family. Not surprisingly, it is also his pattern for life within the family of God; that is, it is a pattern for Christian discipleship. In Galatians 5:6, Paul reveals the pattern, saying, "For in Jesus Christ neither circumcision nor uncircumcision has any value. The only thing that counts is faith expressing itself through love." (The RSV says, "faith working through love.") In 2 Timothy 1:13, he rephrases the pattern, saying, "What you heard from me, keep as the pattern of sound teaching, with faith and love in Christ Jesus." God's pattern for the family, simply stated, is *faith working through love*.

When you help a family, look for failures in this pattern. Failure in faith working through love in the family is the root cause of parenting problems.

As pastor-counselor, identify failures in the pattern and help the family identify those weaknesses. Then, help family members work together to weave that positive pattern of Christian discipleship into the fabric of their lives by learning to apply faith working through love in their family. Let's look closer at this pattern of Christian discipleship.

Love

Love is defined as valuing and avoiding devaluing others. Jesus is our model of love. Jesus laid down his life for us, *while we were still sinners*. He didn't wait until we deserved his love. In Matthew 13:45–46, Jesus said, "The kingdom of heaven is like a merchant looking for fine pearls. When he found one of great value, he went away and sold everything he had and bought it." Jesus is the merchant. Each person is a pearl of value so great that Jesus, the Lord of all creation, gave everything he had to purchase us.

When we love someone, we treat that person as being as important as Jesus thinks he or she is—important enough to give up everything for. We give the person our time, concentration, care, emotional commitment, and resources. We strive never to devalue by putting down or degrading his or her character or work. C. S. Lewis pointed out that everyone was moving either toward a glory so radiant that it cannot be comprehended or toward such hideous ugliness that we would flee in terror if we could comprehend it. When we look at people, we must see their potential, their glory, and avoid treating them as less than image-bearers of God.

Work

When left alone, things degenerate into disorder and confusion. Without receiving energy, a family runs downhill. Without work, a family cannot be healed. Without work, depression, demoralization, and pessimism reign.

Faith

Faith is "being sure of what we hope for and certain of what we do not see" (Heb. 11:1). Jesus Christ is the healer of troubled families and the sustainer of good marriages. We can't see his hand directly, but we can be certain that he cares and always acts to bring about his wonderful plan. In a troubled family it is too easy for vision to be veiled by conflict, anger, distress, disappointment, frustration, and heartache. Painful emotions shroud the glory beyond. Faith for a good family life is multifaceted. Faith in God and his lovingkindness is needed. Faith that people can conform their lives to God's pattern of Christian discipleship—faith working through love—must be present. Faith that effort will yield positive results is required. Faith that pain will eventually end and that counseling can help parents learn to deal with problems more effectively is needed. Faith is a requirement for a course in discipleship.

Faith Working through Love

Within the family, it isn't enough to demonstrate periodic faith, work, and love. Rather, the guiding principle of life—faith working through love—integrates the three elements. Family members show the reality of their faith by working consistently to show valuing love. Children can learn to show such love if they see it directed toward themselves, other family members, people outside the family, and God.

Positive interactions within families are characterized by faith working through valuing love. Negative interactions exhibit a weakness in faith, an unwillingness to work, or a failure in valuing love (which might include actively devaluing a family member). Healthy families need a high ratio of positive faith-working-through-love interactions to negative interactions.

Positive Parenting Is Characterized by Faith Working through Love

Faith Working through Love in Marriage

Life-giving interactions need to outweigh life-draining interactions *substantially* if life is to flourish. John Gottman (1993a, 1993b, 1994) has studied over 2000 marriages intensively in his twenty-plus year research career. His research has a bearing on the whole family as well. Gottman invites troubled and untroubled couples to discuss topics about which they agree and disagree. He videotapes the discussions and monitors partners' physiological responses to each other. Gottman concludes that, in virtually all satisfying, enduring marriages, for every negative interaction partners have, they have five or more positive interactions.

When the ratio of positive-to-negative interactions drops below five-to-one, the marriage changes drastically and significantly. Instead of being characterized by good feelings, positive evaluations of each other and of the marriage, and helpful marriage-strengthening behaviors, the marriage shifts, from Dr. Jekyll-like to Mr. Hyde-like, to one characterized by criticism, defensiveness, emotional withdrawal, and stonewalling (removing oneself emotionally from the marriage). Partners evaluate the marriage as troubled instead of positive or healthy, and each feels frustrated, afraid, angry, distressed, depressed, and hopeless.

Faith Working through Love in the Family

We believe we can extend Gottman's findings from marriage to family life in general. Families have a "feel" to them, as do marriages. The quality of mother-son, father-son, mother-daughter, father-daughter interactions probably depends on the ratio of positive-to-negative interactions between participants. Maintaining a high ratio of positive-to-negative interactions is essential to satisfactory family functioning.

Practicing faith working through love within the family increases the ratio of positive-to-negative interactions. Having faith in each other predisposes each family member to look through rose-colored glasses to expect and find the best amid troubles (see 1 Cor. 13). Working on the relationship prevents the ratio of positive-to-negative interactions from declining, leading to a change in glasses from rose-colored to dark. Practicing valuing love allows family members to feel appreciated and important. Being valued enhances self-esteem, reduces defensiveness and hostile criticism of others, and promotes positive feelings that prevent family members from feeling like cold stone walls. Eliminating devaluing interactions reduces criticism, defensiveness, and emotional withdrawal.

Faith Working through Love in Parenting

Parents lead the family. Their interactions with their children and with each other must demonstrate faith working through love if the family is to flourish. If parents are having trouble with their children, any turnaround must usually come from the parents. Through changing their own behavior, parents stand the best chance of helping their children change.

As the parents' pastor, teach them discipleship—faith working through love. In so doing, you not only help them solve their parenting problems, but you also help them become better disciples of Jesus and function better as members of Jesus Christ's body. This is an exciting and worthy call to you—one in which you can affect generations of Christians.

How to Promote Faith Working through Love in the Midst of Family Conflict

The Problem Isn't Conflict

When family members live together, disagreements will happen. The mere presence of differences screaming for resolution doesn't cause problems. Problems are due to how families handle differences and resolve conflicts.

Not all parenting problems involve conflict, but conflict usually is present when there are parenting problems—conflict between both parents and a child, between one parent and child, between parents concerning how to rear their child, or between two or more children. Let's consider conflict and how to deal with it.

A watershed is the highest elevation on a hill that determines which way water will run off of a hill. Conflict is the watershed of family life. How family members handle conflict—by applying the principle of faith working through love or by failing in faith, work, or love—will aim the family in the direction of love or disintegration.

The Problem Isn't Lack of Knowledge

Conflict is powerful. Conflict stimulates self-justification. Faith working through love opposes self-justification. If a family is to remain intact, members must transcend conflict-inspired self-justification thinking and use faith-working-through-love thinking instead.

It is not merely knowing the principle of faith working through love that returns family members' attention to pursuing love. Mere knowledge rarely determines the direction of interpersonal relationships. If knowledge alone were crucial, psychologists—who have lots of knowledge about families—would not personally have many marital or family troubles, yet psychologists are at high risk for divorce and family turmoil. Why? Psychologists are usually trained in a worldview that promotes self-justification.

The Problem Is Self-Focus

Any family will have numerous disagreements. The essential task is to put aside self-focus and to put others' needs before our own, as Christ did (Phil. 2:4–11). This other-focus helps return the family from negative conflict to positive equilibrium. Faith working through love is laying down our lives for each other, valuing others above our own needs and desires, and working, with Christ's help, to meet each other's needs.

The Problem Is Also a Need for Transformation

If a family is already primarily negative, turn it around. A negative family will worsen until it fragments unless something dramatic happens.

Something can happen within the family to refocus the family members' attention on faith working through love. More likely, though, something must come from *outside* the family to turn the tide. If change is to occur, someone will need to intervene. That someone can be Jesus Christ. Jesus might use a friend or extended family member to speak his message of faith, work, and love to the family. Jesus might use you, the pastor-counselor.

Jesus' intervention is like a personal conversion. It can be dramatic, like an addict throwing down the needle or flushing a stash of cocaine down the toilet. More often, though, conversion represents a change of direction, like repentance. Repentance is turning one's back on sin and walking in the opposite direction. Repentance is like a person walking from his or her home in Richmond toward Atlanta. The person repents, stops ten miles outside of Atlanta, turns, and heads back to Richmond. The person is still ten miles from Atlanta, and there are many miles to travel before arriving home, but the person is moving in the right direction. Eventually, through faith, work, and love, the person will arrive home.

In troubled families, family members often focus on problems and glory in each others' failures. Have hope. Jesus can turn things around through his direct intervention or through sending his ambassador to carry his message of faith, work, and love. (See Table 3–1.)

Table 3–1
Some Possible Beliefs about Parenting

Some Unhelpful Beliefs	Some Helpful Beliefs
Whenever my child disagrees, it is a direct challenge to my authority.	I can have faith that Jesus will help me with my parenting.
Don't get mad, get even.	Forgive those who wrong you. Confess your sins to those whom you have wronged.
Keep score. Everyone should live up to his or her obligations. If I put a lot into the family, I deserve to get a lot out of it.	Be willing to lay down your life for your family.
If it doesn't work out, end the relationship.	Never tire of working on the relationship.
If I'm not appreciated, I should not have to appreciate others. If I am devalued, I am within my rights to devalue.	Value your family members. Don't devalue them.

Revisiting Mary Rae and Marita

The Fundamental Problem

In the vignette with which we opened the chapter, Mary Rae was exasperated with Marita. Marita disobeyed. Mary Rae criticized and devalued. Both were constantly upset. Both had dark glasses on and could see nothing good in their relationship. Problems indicated both Marita's and Mary Rae's failures in faith working through love.

Failures in Love

Marita did not value her mother by being honest with her, obeying the curfew, refraining from drinking, or listening to her mother's concern. She talked back to her mother and treated her mother as someone who needed a brain transplant. She insulted and belittled her mother, sometimes speaking about her mother's weaknesses to her friends within her mother's hearing.

Mary Rae didn't value Marita either. She had increasingly restricted Marita, didn't allow Marita to make decisions, made confining rules, and imposed restrictive punishments when Marita failed to respond to her. She treated Marita as immature, and she justified her behavior by saying that Marita acted immaturely. She discussed her problems with friends, allowing Marita to overhear the conversations. She called Marita names and criticized her every decision. Marita's and Mary Rae's behaviors and attitudes were not loving. Both felt justified in their actions and could cite mounds of evidence to support their positions.

Failures in Work

Marita had given up hope that her mother could ever love her. She counted the days until she could get out from under Mary Rae's oppressive thumb. Rather than try to make the relationship better, Marita was content to ignore her mother and try to avoid punishment as much as she could without having to change her lifestyle much. She didn't try to work toward a solution.

Mary Rae had run the gauntlet of emotions. She had enlisted prayer support from her church, sought counseling from the school counselor and her pastor, read self-help books, watched child-rearing experts on television, and listened to experts on the radio. She had tried a thousand potential solutions to help her daughter mature. None seemed to work. Frustrated and depressed, Mary Rae looked forward to the time when Marita would move out. She gave up working on the relationship.

Failures in Faith

For Marita, faith in Jesus represented "her mother's thing." Marita rejected that faith as inadequate and oppressive. She perceived her mother's attempts to "drag" her to church or "make" her attend youth group as power plays, pure and simple, and she was determined to reject those. Religion was one battle that she'd never let her mother win. Marita also had lost faith that the family could be any other way. As far as she was concerned, her mother's repressive attitude always had been and always would be. Marita had no faith that change was possible.

Mary Rae, too, was in a crisis in faith. While she believed in Jesus as Savior and Lord, she had lost confidence in him as being able to change her life and family. She saw her future with Marita as bleak and hopeless. She had no faith that anyone could help—not her own parents, her ex-husband, her friends at church, her pastor, or the most skilled therapist in the world.

Marita's Decision

By 3:00 A.M., Mary Rae was exhausted and so emotionally wrung out she felt like a dirty dish rag. *Give it up*, every part of her said. *Give it up*, every part answered. She was afraid of what people would say if she farmed Marita off to her father in Massachusetts, but she had tried everything.

Not everything, a voice inside her prompted. *Remember the new assistant pastor who recently came to church. He's had experience working with teenagers. Maybe I'll see him, and when he can't help, then I'll send Marita to Massachusetts.* With those thoughts mingling with vague scenarios of confrontation, she dropped off to sleep.

$$4$$

Common Parenting Problems

Childhood fears, disobedience and rebellion, school problems, trouble making, sibling rivalry, family fighting, whining, tantrums, and aggression—parents' problems reduce to a root cause: weaknesses in faith working through love. In this chapter we show you how faith working through love is intertwined with each problem parents might confront. In each instance we aren't trying to educate you about the intricacies of childhood psychological disorders, or providing a treatment plan for dealing with each disorder. We show—by addressing common problems—how you can see in any parenting problem the weaknesses of faith working through love, which you can then help parents solve by strengthening the weak areas.

In each problem, weaknesses exist in faith, work, love, and the way that faith is worked out through love. But generally, each problem majors in one weakness—either faith, work, or love—and minors in the others. We have organized the difficulties to parallel that idea.

Primary Weaknesses in Faith

Normal Fear

Fear and anxiety are almost always weaknesses primarily in faith. Faith is "being sure of what we hope for and certain of what we do not see" (Heb. 11:1). Fear is looking into the unseen future and finding, in imagination, not what we hope for but potentially terrible things that we don't see.

John tells us, "perfect love drives out fear" (1 John 4:18b). But it is not our own love that drives out fear. It is Christ's perfect love. Christ died for us, receiving the punishment we deserve, and thus Christians do not need to fear that punishment (v. 18c). Instead of people's *love* casting out fear, it is people's *faith* in Jesus' perfect love that frees us from fears. When people experience normal or abnormal fears, a weakness in their faith has generally produced the fear.

Parents, especially parents of first or only children, often are afraid. They don't know what to expect as their children age. They may be troubled that the child is having a serious problem when the child is merely going through a normal adjustment. They may worry about the impact of the decisions they make about discipline and support on their child's later life. Give such parents information about what is normal and what isn't and encourage them to trust God to guide, sustain, and nurture them and their children.

Children develop fears, too. Many fears are normal. In every culture, infants from six to eight months old begin to fear strangers. That fear usually peaks at 14 to 15 months and disappears by 18 to 24 months. Such fear is a normal part of brain development. As the child ages, strange faces may frighten him or her. For instance, my bald head and bearded face must look terrifying to one-year-old children, as if my face were upside down. At least that is my rationalization for the frightened responses babies often give to me. (Yes, I know that it doesn't explain why normal adults cover their eyes in terror and run away at my approach; that's a different story.)

Nonnormal Fears

Childhood fears may become exaggerated, disturbing children and parents. Some exaggerated fears might be due to poor maternal attachment (Ainsworth et al. 1978; Belsky 1988; Bowlby 1969). Babies need to be cuddled, held, talked to, read to, played with, and delighted in. In short, they need to be valued. If babies don't receive such valuing, they may become insecure, fearful, or hostile.

Ray and Jody held middle-management positions within the same large company. When Bart was born, Jody took a leave of absence. After three months, she returned to work. The day-care arrangement for Bart looked good to Ray and Jody when they visited the center, but it was inadequate. Overworked child-care employees didn't have much time to share among the children. By Bart's third year, he was fearful, shy, and easily intimidated. Bart had no sense of stability because his career-directed, overworked parents had little time or energy for him at the end of their busy days, nor did the day-care professionals. For Bart, the future was bleak.

When Charlene had Jean, her marriage to Paul was troubled. Plagued by fits of depression, Charlene believed Paul's threat that if Charlene divorced him he would seek custody of Jean. As the marriage worsened, Charlene felt that divorce was inevitable. She distanced herself from Jean to ease the pain of losing her when she divorced Paul. After several months of Charlene's coldness, Jean began to cry violently whenever Charlene left her. The crying, sometimes lasting two hours or more, went far beyond normal separation anxiety. Eventually, Charlene realized that her distancing conveyed insecure attachment to Jean. When she got marriage counseling she felt more confident about her long-term relationship with Jean. She spent more time with Jean—showing valuing love, cuddling, reading to her, talking to her, playing with her—and Jean's separation fears soon stopped.

Phobias are exaggerated fears of something specific. One of our children was terrified of dogs. She was attacked by a large dog and the fear became full-blown. Her fearful behavior threatened dogs, which made them bark more, which increased her fears even more. Like other fears, phobias are irrational weaknesses in faith, in which the phobic person fantasizes terrible consequences, becomes frightened, and fears losing control (which increases the fear even more).

Phobias are treated successfully in almost 95 percent of the cases through desensitizing the child to what he or she fears. Usually, the child imagines himself or herself in mildly frightening situations and then gradually imagines more fearful situations. Then the child actually exposes himself or herself to mildly fear-provoking situations, under adult care. Gradually, the child learns that he or she does not need to fear. In young children whose imaginations are not well developed, parents can desensitize their children to phobic fears by gradual guided exposure and by parental modeling. (Importantly, the child should *never* be exposed to scary situations with a sink-or-swim attitude.) The Christian parent can combine desensitization with teaching about God's protection and providence.

Disobedience and Rebellion

Direct disobedience is a problem in faith because in it the child learns how to deal with other legitimate authorities by the way the child is allowed to treat his or her parents. When the child learns that he or she can disrespect authorities without negative consequences, the child has been done a disservice. His or her capacity for faith has been damaged. James Dobson (1994), in *The New Dare to Discipline*, describes the necessity of dealing with children's rebelliousness.

Parents often create a disobedient child because they're afraid to discipline the child. They know that a household of warmth and support predict high self-esteem and emotional adjustment in children, but they don't understand that firm control is as necessary to love as is warmth and support. Firm and fair discipline creates opportunities for positive interaction and reduces the number of negative interactions between parents and children, contributing directly to feelings of warmth and support. (Of course, strict discipline alone, without at least five times as much positive parent-child interaction, will not produce happy families.)

Not every disobedient act is rebellion. Barbara, two years old, wants to tie her own shoes. When her mother tries to help, Barbara cries, "I do it." That isn't rebellious disobedience. It's healthy maturity. Children need to be encouraged to do things on their own as they become able. However, if Barbara defiantly kicks her feet and screams "No," or if she throws herself to the floor after her mother has told her that such behavior won't be tolerated, then Barbara is being stubbornly rebellious. Her mother should recognize that Barbara has figuratively spit in her mother's eye and challenged her authority. Barbara's mother must deal with the tantrum firmly.

The late-night conflicts between Marita and Mary Rae over curfew and drinking provide another example of disobedience and rebellion. Both were demoralized. Marita felt unappreciated and unvalued. She saw no possibility of her mother understanding her or changing in the future. Her faith was weak. Mary Rae's faith was weak, too. She felt that Marita had rejected her basic values, one of the most difficult experiences for any parent. Mary Rae felt devalued, discouraged, demoralized, and depressed.

Weaknesses in Work

School Problems

Many—but not all—problems at school and with authorities are weaknesses in work. Often, children who have been belittled and devalued for poor performance or effort or those who can't meet their parents' high standards may begin to fail at school. Their failure may reflect low effort because they'd rather fail by not trying than try and discover they're failures. Choosing not to try gives a sense of control; being stupid is out of their control. Therefore, to maintain a sense of control, some children intentionally quit working.

Other school problems in children occur because parents do not exert the energy, time, and attention to their children's school performance to reward good performance. Paying attention to and praising the child's efforts when he or she does homework each night, studies for tests, completes long-term projects on time, and handles interpersonal conflicts among peers requires enormous effort from parents. Many parents, exhausted by their own struggles at work or at home, don't have the energy to help the child. So they leave the child on his or her own and the child feels, "Why bother working hard. No one notices or cares." If the child only gets attention for failing, he or she may prefer even negative attention to no attention.

Trouble Making

Children want attention, acceptance, and valuing love from their parents. Often they will self-destruct to get a parent's attention. If they can't earn positive attention, they can always get negative attention through causing trouble. Some children shoplift, cheat on examinations, fight, drink, and disrupt classes—all to get their parent's attention. Their problem is not failure to work. They are working hard—at self-destruction.

Parents may contribute to such trouble making in their children without realizing it. Seeing their children reject their values, parents may try to isolate themselves emotionally from the child. Caring hurts, so they quit caring. But by trying to protect themselves they emotionally cut the child off, making the child hunger even more for attention. The child tries harder to gain a response from the parent, and self-destruction spirals upward. Weaknesses in work of parent and child feed each other.

The solution? Parents must find something positive for which to praise the child, have fun with the child, help the child, and engage the child positively. That takes work.

Sibling Rivalry

Similar to trouble making, sibling rivalry is competition for one or both parents' attention. Generally, sibling rivalry is an example on the children's part of misguided effort, in which the children put enormous effort and emotional investment into competing against a sibling. This removes effort from other aspects of their life that are important but aren't directly opposed to the sibling's characteristics.

Sibling rivalry may occur despite what parents do or don't do. Parents can make rivalry worse by placing a lot of attention on the rivalry or by ignoring it, or parents can minimize sibling rivalry by pointing out where each child excels and by downplaying comparisons between the children.

Family Fighting

Family fighting may occur between children, between parents, or between parents and children. A certain amount of bickering and disagreement are to be expected in any family (and may even help family members create clear boundaries and learn healthy conflict resolution), but prolonged, frequent, or harmful fighting are signs that something has gone awry in the family.

Good conflict-management skills can be learned regardless of the person's temperament, background, or current stress. Numerous books, audiotapes, and videotapes exist that show people how to manage disagreements effectively. Thus, in one clear way, the presence of chronic conflict within the family is a product of not placing sufficient effort (work) into finding resources, learning conflict-management skills, and practicing those skills.

On another level, though, chronic conflict is usually an effort to resolve a power struggle. Knowledge alone won't resolve any ongoing power struggle. The essence of a power struggle is a disagreement not over some issue, but over who has the say about the issue. For example, suppose two children disagree over what television show the children want to watch. Each enters the struggle as if this decision were the most important issue in the history of family life. Parents may think they can solve the family disagreement by simply stepping in and making the decision. Not likely. The real problem is fundamental disagreement over *who can say* how decisions are made, who has the power to dominate, who can decide whether to compromise, who can say whether one person will submit.

In a power struggle between the two children, if one child suggests a compromise, the compromise may sound logical to the parent, but at the deeper level the child who proposed the compromise is *saying* how the problem is resolved. The other child will probably reject the suggestion—even if it is a good one. If the parent suggests a compromise—for example, that the family reads instead of watches television—then both children may reject the suggestion or grudgingly accede. Importantly, in either case, the power struggle will not be resolved by simply compromising on particular issues. The children will not have solved the basic issue: who can say.

Power struggles can be resolved by the participants becoming convinced that they have *sufficient* control, *sufficient* value, without having continually to struggle to be top dog by having the final say on each issue. Parents cannot solve children's chronic fighting by imposing clever compromises or giving arbitrary orders. Commands and oppressive authority make the parent feel better but rob both children of control and will only make the children's struggle for power worse. Stern commands from parents may drive family fighting under a cloak of secrecy, which is not what the parent wants but is what the parent is often willing to settle for.

As pastor, you can't solve chronic family fighting by arriving at clever compromise solutions on each of the family's disagreements. You can't impose harmony by invoking biblical authority. Neither action will solve a power struggle. However, those actions may stop the family from seeking your help or it will stop the family from *showing* you that they are still locked in a power struggle.

Resolving power struggles involves helping family members develop the faith that trusts God enough not to require *winning* to prove one's worth. It also involves creating an environment of valuing love, which promotes security. Mostly, though, it involves work at helping family members tirelessly recognize when they are seeking power and demanding their rights. They must respond in love, laying down their own rights, valuing each other, and turning the struggles over to the Lord. Jesus laid down his rights to be equal to God, the Father, and he laid down his life for us (Phil. 2:6–8). Help both adults and children learn to give up their own rights out of love for each other. That is mature discipleship.

Weaknesses in Love

Whining

Whining is nasal, nerve-gangling, noxious complaint. At root, whining says, "People don't appreciate my value. I'm treated unfairly. Don't these people know who I am (the center of creation). I deserve better treatment. I demand my way." As such, whining is a problem in misunderstanding love. It focuses on love received, not love given. Young children are naturally egocentric. They need some sense of self so they can learn that they are different from others. But children don't need to whine to learn that they have a separate identity.

Whining is best dealt with by giving children attention for positive behavior and by ignoring whining. Coach a parent to tell the whining child, "If you whine, I won't give you what you want." If the whining grates on the parent's nerves, the child can be given a "time out," in which the child is removed from all attention—perhaps by seating the child in the corner facing the wall for five minutes. Not only does a time out provide an unpleasant experience for the child, it sometimes preserves the parent's temper. Helping children whine less trains them to avoid whining-like behavior that will cause them problems later in life. When children whine, parents can help (especially older) children understand more about agape love—that people need to think of others when they make choices.

Tantrums

Tantrums, like whining, are problems in valuing love. The child wants his or her way and uses force and emotional intimidation to get it. The child is not living in love by valuing others. Parents may not be responsible for tantrums happening, but they bear some responsibility if they allow tantrums to continue. Tantrums continue only if parents inconsistently deal with the tantrums or parents reinforce the tantrum by giving in to the child. From the beginning, the parent must resolve not to give the tantruming child his or her way. Despite the child's screams and tears or the parent's exhaustion and stress, a loving parent will stop tantrums immediately and consistently, but NEVER by giving the child his or her way.

Behavioral psychologists tell us that tantrums are best dealt with by ignoring the tantrum. However, this involves much more than simply pretending the child is not there whenever she tantrums. Three-year-old Susie tantrumed regularly when she was told to pick up her toys. She refused to pick up. If Millie insisted, Susie dawdled, exasperating Millie. If Millie told Susie to pick up faster, Susie threw toys at her toy box, slammed drawers, and kicked furniture. If Millie scolded, Susie cried and screamed. Millie was frustrated because the house was always a wreck, so she straightened the house after Susie went to bed.

Here's how Susie's mother stopped Susie's tantrums. Millie's pastor convinced her that she was not loving Susie by allowing Susie to disobey by throwing tantrums. Millie got past her own excuses. "It's not so bad. It's just a phase. She'll get over it. Maybe I'm too harsh." Millie decided that Susie must learn to obey and not emotionally blackmail others.

Millie started tantrum-busting early in the afternoon—just after Susie's snack when Susie was fresh and content. Millie hoped that Susie would obey instantly, so she could be rewarded by a special activity. She told Susie, "Honey, pick up your toys in your room and in the living room. When they are put away, you can help me make cookies."

Susie whined that she didn't want to pick up. She scuttled over, hugged Millie's leg, and gave her an "adorable" look. Millie was resolute. "Honey, pick up your toys so we'll have time to make cookies."

Susie objected louder. Millie took Susie by the shoulders and helped her into the living room. "First, pick up that, that, and that"— she pointed to each toy—"and take them to your room and put each one in its place." Millie watched Susie reluctantly pick up one toy.

"Great! Run and put it up. See how fast you can get the others," said Millie, returning to the kitchen. Susie didn't come out of her room for a minute. Millie investigated and found Susie playing with a hat and purse. "No, honey," said Millie, "no playing until all toys are put away."

Millie led Susie back to the living room, and Susie began to scream. Millie kneeled and looked into Susie's contorted face. Holding her shoulders, she said, "Susie, you can cry and scream all you want. I'm not going to pay any attention to it. But you can't play until all of your toys have been put away. I want to fix cookies with you. I hope we'll have time."

When Millie turned Susie loose, Susie hit the ground screaming. Millie went back to work. After ten minutes, the cries trickled off. Millie returned to the living room. "Are you finished crying? Good. Now pick up your toys and put them in their proper places. If you hurry, we may still be able to make cookies." Susie began to scream again. Millie returned to the kitchen without a word.

By 5:30, Susie was exhausted, and Millie's nerves were frazzled. Susie still lay on the floor. Millie heard no sound, and she went immediately to the living room. Susie was beginning to doze. Kindly, Millie picked Susie up. "Are you tired, honey? Let's wash your face with cold water. It's not time to sleep. You haven't put your toys away."

Millie gently washed Susie's face and said, "I know it's hard, but you must learn to put your toys away when Mommy says to. I wanted us to fix cookies this afternoon, but we didn't have time. Let's put those toys away before dinner. Dinner will be on the table in fifteen minutes. I'll set the buzzer. See if you can put all your toys away before the buzzer goes off."

Susie moved the toys to the bedroom floor. She came to the kitchen and told Millie that she was finished. "Good," said Millie. "Just in time for dinner. Let's see what your room looks like."

The room was a shambles. "Oh, honey, remember, you need to put your toys on their shelves, not dumped on the floor. Better get to work. Dinner is almost ready, and the buzzer is about to go off."

Susie hit the ground again. Millie picked Susie up and looked into her face again. "Honey, you already missed the cookies because you wasted time by crying. I'm not going to pay any attention to your crying, but if you don't finish picking up your toys by the time we have finished dinner, then you won't be able to eat dinner with us tonight. It's up to you."

Susie crumbled to the floor.

Millie was always supportive, always kind, never harsh or devaluing. Yet she was always firm in sticking to her ultimatum. She was prepared to have Susie miss dinner if Susie insisted, and she was also prepared to resume the battle the following morning before breakfast if that was necessary. It wasn't. Most children are bright enough to spot their parents' resolution. Susie was, and she only challenged Millie one other time with a tantrum, which Millie again handled with kind but firm resolve.

Aggression

An aggressive child values his own wants above consideration of others. The main problem is one of love. The aggressive child may hit or bully other children or even the parents. Loving parents won't let aggressiveness continue. They must value their child enough to prevent the child from getting his or her way by using aggression. Research has shown that aggression in children has been associated with five factors (Berger 1988):

- undeveloped empathy (the child can't see from another's perspective)
- poor academic or physical performance leading to poor self-esteem
- feeling anger at situations the child can't change
- viewing television and movie violence
- seeing aggression modeled at home

These break down into three main ideas. First, children might have difficulty valuing others and themselves. Second, they encounter situations that prompt anger. Third, they have observed and copied violent ways of dealing with anger.

The second and third groups are almost unavoidable in today's society. Models of violence are everywhere—on television, in movies, on videotaped movies shown in the home, in the schools, and in many domestic interactions. Parents can minimize their children's observation of such violence, but they can't eradicate it. There will always be frustrations. Parents can't eliminate bad happenings, but they can model nonaggressive ways to handle frustration. Teaching love—willingness to value others—is the only real hope of reducing violence substantially. Pastors can help parents teach their children how to see things from others' perspectives and to feel better about themselves when they practice such altruism. Both esteem of others and self-esteem can be promoted through parents teaching their children how to love.

Summary

The main principle of this book—that parenting, which is a form of discipleship, depends on faith working through love—is simple but profound. It is easy to understand but requires daily practice and commitment. Counseling based on this principle is flexible and can be applied to many problems if you but look.

We began the chapter by saying that we hoped to show you that you could recognize failures in faith, work, and love in problems about which parents will often consult you. We talked little of the specific solutions to the problems because we first wanted you to become more adept at using the reasoning of faith working through love to analyze problems. In the following chapter, we examine the strategic solution to problems in faith working through love.

5

The Strategic Solution to Parenting Problems

Two streams join into one at the mouth of a river. At points along the river's path, other tributaries join the river. The water flows, rushing here, languishing there, dipping in sink-holes, splashing over rapids, plunging from waterfalls, churning at times in backwater eddies that seem to go nowhere, but forever moving toward its destination. When a mighty river, like the Mississippi, reaches its destination, it branches into a fertile delta and then dumps its water into the sea.

As the river flows oceanward, it inevitably passes through valleys and rolls over snags. The snags may collect debris until the river is dammed up. Once dammed, the water rises and pressures mount against the dam. The river spreads, seeking a place of weakness to burst through. If the dam remains intact, though, the spreading flood can ruin surrounding areas, creating the vast devastation of eroded farm land, destroyed buildings, and mud everywhere.

Family life is like a river. Two branches merge into one flesh at marriage. At various points along the path of the marriage, children join like tributaries swelling the banks of the family. As the family ages, there are times of energetic rushing to and fro, sink-holes of

69

discouragement, fun-filled rapids that rush by all too fast, exhilarating waterfalls of excitement, and times of stagnation that swirl seemingly without purpose. Yet always the family moves toward the time when the tributaries will separate from the main body. At last, the couple, like a river stripped of its tributaries, will move together to a heavenly destination.

Inevitably along the way, the family will run into snags that dam the smooth flow. Dams are usually encountered within the valleys of life. Snags collect debris, which further gum up the works, until the dam may be a giant obstruction to the flow of the family river. If the dam is not broken, pressures mount and water backs up and spreads into other areas of life, contaminating, seeking weaknesses to batter, destroying valuable fertile plans for the future, eroding memories, and knocking down the structures that the family took so long to build. Finally, even if the dam is broken, mud-stained memories blacken the countryside.

One solution to the dam's destructiveness is to build a dynamo that can use the power of the dammed-up water constructively. Ideally, the entire region will be helped through harnessing the water's power.

The pastor is the engineer who helps the family design the dynamo. The engineer establishes a relationship with the family that provides the motivation to work to solve the problem. The engineer helps assess the problem so that the family can build the best dynamo to accomplish their goals. The engineer then helps design the plans, but the family must carry out the labor of love in faith that actually builds the dynamo. The pastor helps build channels through the dam that can direct the water over turbines to generate power.

The pastor's work is both remedial and preventive. It solves current problems and prevents future ones. Finally, the pastor, through promoting forgiveness, helps the family clean up the mess caused by the dammed up river.

The Problem

Ideally, the family is the best place for meeting one's important needs. Trying to meet their needs for meaning through gaining a sense of effectance (the ability to produce desired effects) and intimacy, family members encounter obstacles to faith, work, and love. When needs for meaning are not met, problems in faith arise. When needs for effectance are not met, problems in work arise. When needs for intimacy are not met, problems in love arise. Family members can deal with these problems effectively or ineffectively.

Effective solutions involve applying God's discipleship principle, faith working through love, to the obstacles. Ineffective application of the discipleship principle produces enduring family problems. Generally, the children have a weakness in faith, work, or love that shows up as a problem, and the parents have a related problem in faith, work, or love that shows up as a problem in parenting.

The Solution

To solve the family's problems, parents must replace ineffective weaknesses in faith, work, and love with effective parenting and teach their children to act in faith, work, and love, too. In this way, discipleship is built within the family (see Lee 1991 for other suggestions about building disciples within the family).

The pastor can disciple parents into applying effective faith-working-through-love solutions. Where there are problems in faith, the pastor must promote hope. Where there are problems in work, the pastor must promote a willingness to try to change and a persistence to work. Where there are problems in love, the pastor must promote the willingness to value each other. To the extent the pastor can promote hope, motivation to work, and willingness to value each other, respectively, the family members can experience a renewed sense of meaning, effectance, and intimacy.

Parents can learn to analyze and deal with parenting problems by applying a five-step method. We use AGAPE as an acrostic to help parents remember how to deal with problems in faith working through love.

- *Assess:* Parents analyze the nature of the problem in terms of the degree to which they need to strengthen faith, work, and love. They get a sense of the difficulty of the problem and the degree of effort needed to handle the problem well.

- *Goal Plan:* Parents decide what needs to be done to make the problem better. They describe those actions in clear terms. Those solutions become goals for the parents to work toward in faith and love.
- *Act:* Parents then take actions aimed at reaching their goals. They try to make changes that promote discipleship in themselves and their children.
- *Persevere:* Parents must persevere despite times when they cannot easily see progress. Change requires work and faith that if they continue to build each other up in love, the problems will lessen and more positive experiences will happen.
- *Evaluate:* Parents must continually evaluate how well they are achieving the goals they set earlier. If the parents are not making satisfactory progress, they must adjust their actions and persevere until change occurs.

Parents learn this method of analyzing and dealing with their parenting problems in approximately the third session of counseling, and they apply it to numerous problems after they have learned the method.

Characteristics of Faith-Working-through-Love (Discipleship) Parenting

Disclose to parents a style of parenting that has four primary characteristics. The parents' behavior will be (1) oriented toward a Christian vision of the family, (2) child-focused, (3) unified (both parents acting in concert), and (4) positive.

Discipleship parenting is based on a Christian vision of the family. Instead of a peace-at-any-price mentality, parents should have Jesus' mentality. He is more concerned about our relationship with him than about whether we have peace and pleasure. Help parents develop the mindset that their God-given task is to build disciples of Christ—to mold their children's character, even if sometimes the parents won't have peace and pleasure.

Second to being Christ-centered, discipleship parenting is child-focused. A Christian view of parenting is focused on love, which puts others' needs above our own. To apply this principle consistently, parents need to learn about children and their changing needs at different ages, and parents need to focus their energy, not on their own happiness, but on their children's discipleship. In the end, parents will feel happy because they diligently train their children.

Discipleship parenting is unified. Children respond best to a united front rather than to being tugged in different directions. Even if parents disagree on fundamental values, they can agree on many child-rearing attitudes and policies.

Discipleship parenting is positive. Happiness and stability in the family depends on having more interactions that promote faith working through love than negative interactions. Problems focus attention on the negative. Parents must focus on solutions. They can learn to be positive and to notice and praise even the smallest progress.

The Pastor's Tasks

Strategic counseling for parenting problems involves a series of goals.

- Establish a good working relationship.
- Assess problems and show how they indicate weaknesses in faith working through love.
- Teach parents the strategy of discipleship.
- Help parents see the seeds of their current behavior in their own parents' behaviors.
- Help parents plan specific actions that employ faith working through love to prevent future problems.
- Consolidate the learning from the pastoral counseling and help the parent terminate counseling.

To accomplish these tasks, you need to understand four things:

- the basic principle of faith working through love, and how to employ it to discern causes and solutions for parenting problems
- how to conduct the Encounter, Engagement, and Disengagement stages of Strategic Pastoral Counseling for parenting problems

- how to carry out each of the five sessions of Strategic Pastoral Counseling as applied to parenting problems
- how to apply the three stages of Strategic Pastoral Counseling with common parenting problems

Techniques or Strategies?

When I began to counsel almost 20 years ago, I longed for powerful counseling techniques that I could lift almost verbatim from a book and apply with the people I was trying to help. I hoped that those techniques would make a life-changing impact on those in my care.

It didn't happen that way often. I was usually more excited about using counseling techniques than my clients were about having them applied to them. Over the years, I have all but abandoned the search for the magic pill that will cure the ailing family. I don't believe that families are helped by "counseling techniques," no matter how classy. Parents benefit by the counselor's *love*, care, and prayer for the client as the counselor *works* with the client and displays *faith* that God is sovereign and can change the lives of anyone regardless of how desperate the person's situation. In other words, the pastor who is effective at counseling lives the principle of discipleship. Techniques don't cure. Cure comes through Jesus Christ working via relationships that rely on him and God's Word.

Troubled families, too, want a magic pill. You can't provide it. You can only help families turn to Jesus Christ and submit themselves to him and to God's biblical pattern of discipleship—faith working through love. That is the strategic solution for both pastor and parents.

Part 2

Faith-Working-through-Love Parenting

6

Christian Vision-Oriented Parenting

Like all parents, I have not always been a stellar example of good Christian parenting. We went through a difficult period in which Jonathan was not performing academically in a way that satisfied me or him. The problem wasn't intelligence. Jonathan is very bright. But he didn't seem to want to study enough to do well.

I was reared by parents who stressed the importance of working hard to get a good education, so Jonathan's unwillingness to study was like waving a red flag in front of me. I can still remember the confrontations when grades arrived home—rising heat in my face, roaring blood in my ears, thumping heart, feeling as if my stomach and head would explode.

And explode I did. I fussed and fumed. It didn't produce any higher grades for Jonathan, but it did produce resentment.

I was also raised to avoid conflict as much as possible. I didn't enjoy those grade-related encounters with Jonathan. In fact, I hated them and what they were doing to my relationship with Jonathan. So, I did what many men do when they feel the heat of rage. I withdrew. I "did turtle," tucking my head firmly in my shell. I avoided my son, fearful that his slightest provocation would send me

77

through the roof. I convinced myself that Jonathan would appreciate my avoidance of conflict.

Finding myself in the bedroom with my head stuck in a book while mentally rehearsing heated conversations with Jonathan, I was confronted by God, who showed me that I, like Jonathan, had many times taken my own, self-destructive track, pulling defiantly away from God's leading, rejecting values that God held dear. Did God get hurt and sulk? Nope. God didn't withhold love with an unexpressed irrational assumption that if he stayed in *his* room, I'd come to my senses! To the contrary, when I pulled away the hardest, God was most available if I wanted to return. I realized that I needed to see what was behind Jonathan's lack of effort. Insecurity, fear of failure, lack of maturity? I needed to encourage Jonathan's efforts and to be available to listen to, help, and pray for him.

Parents Are God's Stewards

Help Children Know God's Character

God established parents to rule and reign over their children as his stewards in his stead. As stewards, we are not little gods. We merely rule *for* him while he is not physically present. Parents should thus try to rule as God would rule, emulating his character, so that the children can know God through the godly behavior of their parents. To the extent that parents can help their children become faithful disciples of Jesus Christ, their parenting will please God.

God Did Not Leave Parents Unequipped

God didn't leave parents clueless about how to parent in a way that reveals his character. He provided great examples in Scripture. He revealed himself as *Father*, the prototype of all parents. God's character as a loving parent leaps from every book, almost every page of the Bible.

Parents Need to Know God

A historian could, from extensive research, describe Martin Luther King, Jr., so vividly that I might be able to feel that I almost "know" him, even though I never met him. But think of the difference if an intimate friend of Martin Luther King, Jr., who had a lifetime of personal experiences with him, shared about King's character. How much more would he come alive.

Parents can teach their children about the living God if they have actually met God through Jesus, God's son, and have a lifetime of personal experiences with him. They can describe the presence of Jesus in the bumps and knocks of their personal past. This doesn't say that all parents who are Christians are better parents than are parents who are not Christians. Rather, parents who are Christians are better parents than they would be if they were not Christians.

The Most Important Task of Parenting

The most important task of parenting is to create disciples of Jesus Christ who know God personally and rely on the Holy Spirit within them to guide their lives. If parents can achieve that goal, many other benefits may follow. Whether children develop to parents' expectations, though, parents will have done what is important as parents.

Others—not always Christians—have suggested that discipleship and discipline share a common Latin root—"learner" (Bettelheim 1987; Eggebroten 1987; Lee 1991; Narramore 1972). As Lee (1991) observes, parents who focus on discipline as punishment will think of ways to stop unwanted behavior, but parents who think of discipline as discipleship will think more about what the child is learning—more about God's character.

How Parents Can Reveal
God's Character to Their Children

God's character blends love and holiness, a desire to communicate, and perfect empathy. Parents can help their children learn about each of these qualities of God.

God's Character: Love and Holiness

Love is shown in grace and mercy. Grace is giving us the good that we don't deserve, and mercy is not giving us the bad that we do deserve. Holiness is setting standards and sticking to them. A blend of love and holiness involves clear rules, clear consequences if rules are obeyed or disobeyed, and valuing love always freely given. Parents can show their children the merciful character of God. That doesn't mean letting the child off the hook repeatedly so that the child learns that there are no consequences for his or her behavior. To the contrary, without consequences there can be no mercy. If some acts did not deserve punishment, there would be no freedom to choose and no opportunity for a merciful God to grant mercy.

Martin Luther wrote that the Ten Commandments were simultaneously law and prophesy. "You shall have no other gods before me. . . . You shall not covet." The laws guide behavior and also describe our coming life in heaven with God when none of the commandments will be broken and joy and worship will reign. Similarly, parents understand that their standards are simultaneously guidelines for their children's behavior and descriptions of a family in which the children abide by the guidelines. Parents aren't pleased by punishment. They long to praise obedience. By having clear and fair guidelines that guide conduct in their household and provide occasions for praise, parents can enjoy a home characterized by discipline, order, and love.

God's Character: Communication

God tells people about himself because he longs to know them and to be known by them. He clearly communicates a consistent message through word and deed. He established prayer to provide an opportunity for people to talk to him and for him to listen and talk to us. He gave the Scriptures and the Holy Spirit as ways of talking to people and allowing them to listen to him.

Parents can emulate God's communication. Encourage parents to set regular opportunities for children to talk and parents to listen and vice versa. Help parents build such times into a family's life from the time that children are young. But even if parents did not establish open communication with their young children, they can do so later.

God's Character: Empathy

God wants people to know that he understands them and that they can identify with him. So, in the ultimate act of empathy, God became human in the person of Jesus. He laid down equality with God the Father and took a body, endured temptation without yielding to it, suffered from the stress of people clamoring for more of his time and energy than his human body was capable of giving, felt the bloodless wound of interpersonal rejections, felt frustration when the lessons he taught were ignored by the people he lived with and taught daily, watched in disappointment as his children ran away from him when he was in trouble, and felt gratification as he hung crucified and watched his loved ones come to the foot of the cross. Jesus understands and empathizes with the plight of the parent.

Empathy is understanding the thoughts and feelings of another while remaining cognizant of one's own thoughts and feelings. Jesus understands people while maintaining his God-nature. Parents, too, can enter into the perceptual world of the child, feeling with the child and understanding the child's thoughts, while maintaining a higher understanding of the child's behavior and its consequences. Empathy provides a point of contact between parent and child. It provides a starting point for the parent to enter the life of the child and communicate meaningfully with the child. The child can learn to understand the parent if the parent can begin empathically to show that he or she can understand the child.

Teaching God's Character

While good character is often "caught," it is also taught. Jesus was a wonderful teacher. He often taught using interesting stories tailored exactly to his audience. Often, the stories had one meaning on the surface but had deeper significance, too, for those who could understand. Parents should not shy away from teaching—either directly or through stories. Their stories need not always be moral fables or parables but should be interesting and should be tailored to the interests of their children.

How Can the Pastor Help Parents
Develop a Christian Vision of Parenting?

Begin with the Parent's Experience

Mary Rae (from Chapter 3) arose bleary-eyed from lack of sleep. Marita had stumbled to the bus just in time, obviously still feeling some effects of the alcohol she had drunk the night before. Mary Rae felt guilty letting Marita go to school still somewhat under the influence, but Mary Rae felt that she *had* to do something about the problem. *Our new assistant pastor, Pastor John, is a God-send*, thought Mary Rae.

She slurped the last of her third cup of coffee and dumped into the sink some grounds that had worked their way past the filter into her cup. She called the church.

At nine o'clock, Mary Rae sat across from Pastor John. Far from feeling comforted, Mary Rae, 41 years old, despaired when she saw the young man of probably 25. *How's he going to tell me anything useful about dealing with Marita? He's closer to her age than to mine*, she thought.

"I'm at the end of my rope," said Mary Rae. "I simply can't handle Marita. I'm going to send her to Massachusetts to live with her father."

Listen Actively

Pastor John said, "You sound as if your mind is made up."

"It is." Mary Rae hesitated. "But it isn't." She gnawed at her lower lip. "I want to be finished with the conflict with Marita so I can forget these bad times, but if I send her to Massachusetts, I'll feel like a loser. I don't know what to do."

Pastor John nodded.

"Last night it seemed so logical to send her away. Today," she shrugged, "it's not so clear."

Mary Rae summarized the constant conflicts between her and Marita. Pastor John listened intently, often reflecting back what Marita had said. After 30 minutes, she wound down.

Pastor John summarized what Marita was facing: "You've had a lot of conflict with Marita. It bothers you when she is rebellious. You don't feel as if she's valuing you. You think that things won't work out, and it makes you want to give up. It's hard to keep a strong faith when you can't see how the situation can improve."

Promote the Parent's Empathy for the Child

"It bothers me—probably more than it should."

"What do you mean?"

"In many ways, I can see myself in her. I was a wild teen, and my parents never could or would restrain me. I fell in with a rough crowd, married Marita's father, and never went to college. We lived in Colorado when I had Marita. Then I became suddenly single and have struggled since. I've always thought that if my parents had sat on me, I wouldn't have had half the pain I've had to endure."

"So, much of the pressure you feel to correct Marita has come from the way you were raised."

"I've never thought of that before but it's true. I guess I'm trying to help Marita avoid my mistakes."

"And how has that worked?"

"Not too well. She's rebelling just like I did. I rebelled because I wanted to be controlled. She seems to rebel because I control her."

Pastor John said, "You didn't feel valued because your parents didn't control you, and Marita doesn't feel valued because you're too controlling?"

"Right."

"It sounds like you can partly understand how she feels."

"I can probably understand exactly. I've made mistakes and want to help her avoid those mistakes, but she won't listen."

"I'm impressed with how much you value Marita. You think that if you can get her to obey, then you can help her have what you didn't have—real family love."

"If she doesn't obey, she's going to self-destruct."

Help the Parent Distinguish
Between Obedience and Discipleship

Pastor John shifted uncomfortably, knowing he was about to challenge Mary Rae. "I sense, though, that getting Marita to obey might not be your complete goal. You seem to want to go beyond obedience."

"What do you mean?"

"Marita can obey you for many wrong reasons. You seem to care about her character, not just her conformity to your rules."

"I am concerned for her character," said Mary Rae. "If she continues to rebel against anything that I or any other authority figure does, then she's going to get in serious trouble."

Pastor John nodded. "You obviously think of her as a pearl of great value. You want to disciple her so that she obeys and at the same time learns good reasons for obedience."

"That would make me ecstatic." She sounded skeptical.

"But you can't believe she can learn good reasons for obedience."

Mary Rae hesitated. "I know she *can* learn, but I can't believe—based on how she's acted lately—that she *wants* to learn."

"So your faith that Marita can learn self-discipline is uncertain."

"Wouldn't you be uncertain?"

Pastor John smiled. "If I had gone through what you've gone through, I'm sure my confidence would be uncertain—despite how hard I wanted to work on the relationship."

"It's been hard."

"I can tell that it has been hard for you. You still want to help Marita become a disciple of Jesus, though, and not merely an outwardly obedient and inwardly rebellious child."

"More than anything."

"And as a disciple, she would obey for the right reasons, not for the wrong reasons—which could happen if you focus on obedience, not discipleship."

Help the Parent Commit to Changing His or Her Own Behavior

Mary Rae sat silent for a while. "I have never really thought about being a parent as if it were helping disciple my child. It's . . . it's a different way of thinking."

"If you think of parenting as helping to train a disciple, then how would that affect the way you parented?"

She lowered her eyes. "I'd stop being so critical and negative, maybe not lose my temper as much. And, I guess, not get so discouraged—maybe take a longer-term view." She straightened a book on Pastor John's table. "I'd probably give more attention to the spiritual consequences of her behavior."

"This is great," said Pastor John. "You seem to be saying that you would treat Marita like Jesus treated his disciples. If you were discipling Marita like Jesus discipled his followers, what would you do?"

"I'd be more interested in teaching her than in punishing her— though I'd have to correct her sometimes like Jesus did with Peter."

Get Specific

"Let's get right to the nitty-gritty. What are you going to do differently as Marita's mother?"

Mary Rae's face fell. She put her hand on her forehead covering her eyes. After a while, she said, "I don't know. It was fun for a minute. I actually got excited about parenting. But thinking about what I would do differently makes me feel hopeless all over again."

"Then let's be systematic. How can you show Jesus' love to Marita today?"

"I guess I should apologize to her for always being on her back, treating her like a child. But—" she quickly held up her hand, "that doesn't mean that her getting drunk and violating curfew was okay. It wasn't."

"Right." said Pastor John. "Marita seemed to be testing the limits or simply disregarding the limits even though she knew what they were."

"She was disregarding them. I've talked with her over and over about both curfew and drinking."

"So how will you walk the line between love and justice, between mercy and responsibility, between holding her accountable for her behavior and supporting?"

Mary Rae was silent for over two minutes. At last, she leaned forward. "Here's what I think I'll do. I'll apologize for being critical of her, and I'll listen to what she thinks about her behavior." She smiled. "Listen. Ha. That'll be such a switch, she'll probably have a stroke. Anyway, after I've listened, I'll ask what she thinks should be done about it."

"What do you think would happen if you told her some of the wild things you did in your youth as a way of explaining your concern for her?"

"She might lose respect for me."

"How's her respect level been lately?"

"Oooh. Good point. I guess I haven't much to lose, do I?"

"Might Marita actually gain respect for you if you shared your concerns and love for her instead of immediately laying into her?"

"You're right."

Over the next 30 minutes, Mary Rae and Pastor John discussed the afternoon's likely encounter. Pastor John carefully framed it in terms of ways that Mary Rae could use herself to show aspects of God's character.

As they wrapped up the one and one-half hour conversation, Pastor John summarized by saying, "The Bible lays out a vision of the family as people who are committed to each other, who sacrifice their own wants for each other's good, who strive to teach and learn Christian discipleship, and who practice faith working through love. The family, with parents at its head, is like the church with Jesus as its head. You are willing to make sacrifices for Marita because you love her. By seeing parenting as disciple-making, you have faith that Jesus will work in her life and in your relationship. You have an excellent plan for the afternoon and a good strategy for the long haul. Call me when you've talked with Marita, and we'll decide whether to meet again."

Table 6–1

Guidelines for Helping Parents See How They Can Promote a Christian Vision of Parenting

- Begin with the child's experience
- Listen actively
- Promote the parent's empathy for the child
- Help the parent distinguish between obedience and discipleship
- Help the parent commit to changing his or her own behavior
- Get specific

Summary

Helping troubled parents develop a Christian-oriented vision for their family is not easy. (See Table 6–1 for a summary.) Parents are usually wrapped up in immediate conflicts and problems. However, when the pastor thinks strategically and has a clear vision of the family, he or she can help parents catch the vision.

7

Child-Understanding Parenting

We have heard hundreds, perhaps thousands, of personal testimonies of people's journey of faith. Many have been thrilling; others more sedate. We've personally identified with many. Though they may have similarities, they are each unique. Their uniqueness testifies to God's plan, which is to treat each person as a valuable human being, individually a pearl of great value and also part of a valuable community treasure house of faithful people.

William Blake wrote,

> I give you the end of a Golden String,
> Only wind it into a ball,
> It will lead you in at Heaven's Gate
> Built in Jerusalem's Wall.

William Blake suggests that the life of faith is like seeing the glint of a golden string in the mud of the world. We are drawn to the glitter, fish it out, sling the slime from it, and begin to coil it into a compact ball. As we collect the string, it draws us on. As we walk, deliberately, step by step, gathering the twine to our bosom, we follow where the string leads. We find that all that glitters isn't necessarily gold but is sometimes more precious and more lasting. The golden string pulls us into surprising places, through mud, across the thrones of royalty, through misty clouds into brilliant sunlight, and back to the prickly thicket. But eventually, if we keep our perspective, we arrive, ball of twine perhaps overbalancing us, sweaty and tired, but full of memories of adventure, at "Heaven's Gate Built in Jerusalem's Wall." And we find that it was worth it.

We have had entirely different experiences with the Lord, yet we've both grown into more maturity in the Lord than we began with. God has tailored experiences specifically for our personalities, making life with him a continual adventure. Although the strings look different, they are attached to the same Lord.

Childhood and the Golden String

Children find their own string. Parents point to the string of faith, guide them in plucking the string of knowledge of Christ from the mud of the world, and perhaps see them uncover a career direction and marriage partner. At first, many children don't know they have a string in their grasp, and they may flounder or may proceed on automatic pilot—doing all the right things but not understanding where they are headed. They may accept Christ early but not understand how to allow him to be Lord and King. Eventually, though—often in high school, sometimes in college, sometimes beyond college—they catch the glint of gold, and they are off and winding.

Parenthood and the Golden String

Being a parent has its mountaintops and valleys, its quicksand and pavement. Parents have the despair of seeing their words bounce off impenetrable skulls and the ecstasy of seeing their children's lives unfold like a kaleidoscope. Through it all, we follow our string as it leads through forests of children's team sports, awards ceremonies, classroom befuddlement, and PTA meetings. Parents inch upward and often hang suspended from the lofty cliffs of their children's achievements, friendships, first dates, and career decisions. Parents weather the droughts of middle school, rejections by children's friends, criticism by their coaches and teachers, and perhaps puppy loves gone to the dogs. Parents slog through the hard undergrowth of emotional ups and downs, failures, our own stressfulness and its effects on our parenting—all the time hoping that we and they will emerge on the other side to a beautiful meadow.

Parents diligently wind in the string of faith, the string of parenting, the string of maturing, only to find that they are wound in as much as they are winding. They reach hilltops, such as seeing their children's high school or college graduation, but the journey, of course, isn't about their reaching hilltops—exhilarating though the view may be at the time. Being a parent is about following one's golden string and seeing one's children's golden strings revealed. It's about professing what parents believe and who they are to the precious ones in their care. Parenting is not easy, but it's what parents do.

Each person's string—child's, parents', pastor's—takes him or her through events that are similar to those in other people's lives. But each person's string is individually molded to fit snugly against the shape of the heart. God is like that.

Tailoring Parenting to the Child

If parents are to emulate God and build loving and effective disciples of Jesus Christ, then they must tailor their parenting to the specific needs of their children. Several ideas are embedded in that statement: (1) parents must decide that they want to emulate God and train loving and effective disciples of Jesus Christ; (2) to tailor parenting to the child, parents must accurately understand their child; and (3) parenting consists of skills that can be fitted to different children.

Parents Can Decide to Emulate God

Many Christians do not think their job is making Christian disciples of their children. They would rather rear children who are nice, hard-working, honest, smart, or ambitious (or many other good characteristics) than rear children who are spiritual. "Sure, religion is important," they might say, "but after all, children have to get along in the world, don't they?"

As pastor, challenge parents to think about their priorities—not just the priorities that they *say* are important, but also the priorities that are revealed by the way they are living. Often, that confrontation won't result in any changes, but sometimes people will honestly evaluate their priorities and will reorder their lives as a result of your gentle, sensitive suggestion for them to consider their values.

Parents Must Understand Their Child

It's hard for parents to look at their children—the products of their own genes with similar personality and body type, with behaviors that reflect on the parent's skill and ability to parent—and understand the child accurately. It's too easy to see oneself in one's children, and it's too hard to judge oneself accurately.

Most parents' unconscious personal ambitions for their children are often hidden, even from the parents. Parents may want their children to excel in some area—not because the child would benefit but because the parent is working out an unresolved problem through the child's performance.

As a child, I tried to earn approval from my parents by succeeding at sports. So, when my children reached an age in which they could play sports, I strongly encouraged them and gloried in their successes. If parents can be helped to look at their parenting in light of their own family-of-origin background, they might uncover some of the conflicts that are driving their parenting. They might find that their child's behavior bothers them because *they*, not their child, find the behavior important.

God wants each of us to develop his or her gifts so that we can glorify God and benefit the body of Christ. He wants us, as the Army slogan puts it so well, to "be all that we can be," so he arranges experiences that are tailored to our personality, temperament, and gifts to help us develop our gifts and our character. God is never going to bask in our glory. Our efforts fall far below his splendor. So his motives are to bring the best out of us that can be extracted. Parents should cultivate that motive. They should not bask in their children's glory but should help the children discover and cultivate the gifts God gave them.

God understands each person. If parents are to emulate God they should seek to understand each child as unique. Encourage the parent to understand the child's uniqueness by asking the parent, (1) "How is the child different from you in personality, temperament, and talents? From your spouse? From both of you?" or (2) "What do you, as an adult, really want to accomplish in your life? Are there ways that you are living your dream through your child?" While asking those questions won't guarantee that parents look at their children without filtering what they see through their own experiences, the questions will often help parents think about the child's uniqueness.

Parents Must Tailor Parenting Skills to Fit the Child

Help the parent develop skills needed to understand his or her child. All parents need parenting skills, but just as a suit that is pulled from the rack may not fit precisely, so parenting skills must be tailored to the child's age, intelligence, background, and temperament. Following are six parenting skills that must be adapted to the child (see Table 7–1).

Table 7-1
Parenting Skills to Adapt to Each Child

1. Develop a mindset of faith working through love
2. Develop parental listening skills
   - Recognize ineffective listening
   - Encourage effective listening
   - Promote good communication in the congregation
3. Develop strategies to prevent misbehavior
   - Forced choices
   - Arrange the home
   - Make expectations clear
4. Develop skills for building positive, Christian values in children
   - Share reasoning with children
   - Bible study with children
   - Christian friends
   - Inoculate
   - Christian stories
   - Discuss hypothetical ("what if . . .") dilemmas
5. Develop skills for using punishment effectively

- Unpleasant, not harmful
- Don't start small and gradually get more severe
- Follow clear standards and consequences
- Have the child repeat
- Praise obedience or follow through with consequences
6. Develop alternatives to punishment
  - Natural consequences
  - Restore damage done by misbehavior
  - Tell the child if the parent is upset

---

1. Develop the mindset of faith working through love. Parents need to see themselves as disciple-makers who practice faith working through love. They need to develop faith-working-through-love glasses through which they can see their decisions. Help them develop such a worldview by including these ideas in sermons, classes, small groups, and informal discussions within the congregation, and when parents seek counseling, let counseling be informed by a discipleship mindset.

2. Develop parental listening skills. Most parents don't listen helpfully to their children. Parents may

- half listen, continuing to work on their own tasks;
- ask specific questions, which may frustrate the child from telling his or her story;
- quickly offer advice;
- deny the child's feelings (for example, the parent may say, "You're making a mountain out of a molehill" or "That's not so bad");
- lecture;
- use logic to defeat the child's suggestions.

Help the parent see that each of these "listening" techniques will inhibit the child from talking, both now and in the future. Describe the unhelpful "listening" techniques to the parents and assign them "homework" of catching themselves if they use any unhelpful listening techniques. Then teach parents positive listening. For example, positive listening includes the following:

- Stop what you are doing, face the child, and listen with undivided attention. Kneel to talk to a small child.

- Encourage the child by saying, "Oh," "I see," "Um," "Right," and the like, which assure the child that you are listening.
- Help the child label feelings. Say, "I see that you're angry."
- Grant a request in fantasy when it isn't possible to grant it in real life. For instance, when Robbie finishes supper, he wants ice cream but none is in the house. "I want ice cream," he says several times. "Okay, one giant dish of make-believe ice cream coming right up for Robbie and his mother." His mother mimes placing a big bowl on his tray. "With a cherry on top," she says. She sits at the table and pretends to spoon the imaginary ice cream in her mouth. "Mmmm. Great stuff. Oops, got some chocolate on my nose. Oh, you have some on yours, too. Better eat up before it melts. Want a cookie to go with it?" She pulls a real cookie from the bag and puts it beside his plate.

In five weeks of pastoral counseling you can't undo a lifetime of poor communication. Nor should you try. That is a prescription for feeling that you have failed as a counselor. Instead, make building better communication within your congregation one goal of your ministry. As parents and others practice faith working through love in their daily lives, many poor communications will disappear.

3. Develop strategies to prevent misbehavior. Help parents develop strategies that encourage their children to behave well. For example, rather than expect that small children will know how to avoid misbehavior, the parent can give forced choices, such as "Do you want to pick up your blocks or your stuffed animals first? After your toys are put away, you can have a snack."

Help parents avoid child misbehavior by arranging the home so that good behavior is likely. For young children, "child-proof" the house by putting breakable and valuable items out of the child's reach. For older children, apply the same principle. In one family, both parents worked until 5:00, leaving the adolescent boy home alone from 4:00 until 5:30 each day. Each morning, the mother and son together devised activities that the boy agreed to accomplish before his father arrived home. The adolescent enjoyed the freedom to monitor his own behavior each day and remain free from having his mother or father supervise his work.

For school-aged children, parents can prevent problems by making their expectations clear. Further, the parent can provide positive suggestions for the child to do rather than offering no guidance and expecting that the child will be resourceful enough to stay out of trouble.

4. *Develop skills for building positive, Christian values in children.* Parents want to build Christian values in their children, but they are often intimidated into not teaching their values under the mistaken belief that they are giving their child a "choice" by not raising them in a Christian home. By not teaching who Christ is and Christian values, parents actually limit children's choices. Certainly public schools and most peers won't provide that information. Children cannot choose Christianity unless they are exposed to it (Rom. 10:14). Most values are caught as much as taught, which makes it important for parents to live as Christians. Parents can promote Christian values in their children in several ways.

- Parents should share their reasoning with their children. If they made a decision based on their Christian values, they should let children see how those values affected their decision making.
- Bible study. Begin when children are small with devotional books or children's versions of the Bible.
- Place children in contact with other Christian children and adults at Sunday school, church, youth activities, and special Christian clubs. Invite Christian friends over.
- As children mature, expose them to non-Christian situations in controlled doses. Like inoculations, which expose the body to a germ and allow antibodies to form, carefully limited "worldly" situations can build resistance against worldly influence if parents discuss those situations and help children analyze the worldly values and choose Christ's plan instead.
- Expose children to positive stories, books, and videotapes (such as narratives of Christian lives, and fiction by C. S. Lewis, Patricia St. John, and others).
- Discuss hypothetical dilemmas within the family. Children can role play situations and decide how they might handle

them. For instance, children can act out how they might react to sexual advances or to being offered drugs by a "friend."

Values are best caught during good family times when parents can notice and encourage positive attitudes and actions. During times of discipline or conflict, children may perceive lengthy parental discussions of Christian values as judgmental and manipulative, which can boomerang. Many values compete for attention and allegiance. Society has lost a Christian consensus, so parents must work diligently to insure that children are raised with Christian values that give them choices in adolescence and early adulthood.

5. *Develop skills for using punishment effectively.* When a parent wants to stop a behavior, punishment is the surest method. Teach parents guidelines for effective punishment.

First, punishment must be unpleasant but not harmful. The child must say to himself or herself, "Do not repeat this experience."

Second, don't start easy and gradually get tougher. That's ineffective. At first the parent tells Susie, "Honey, time to go to bed. Put up your toys." Susie continues to play. The parent, surprised, says, "Susie, maybe you didn't hear. I said, 'Put up your toys and go to bed.'" Trial three: "Susie! Now. The toys." Trial six: "Susan Ellen Smith! (must be serious to use the middle name) Get those toys up." Trial ten: "Susan, my patience is wearing thin. Get those toys up, or I'm going to have to give you a spanking." Trial fourteen: (Screaming) "You are driving me crazy. How many times do I have to tell you? Put those toys away. I mean it." Trial seventeen: "I'm going to count to three and those toys had better be put up. One. Two. Two and one-half. Okay. That's better. Now get to bed." Trial twenty: "Susan, I can't believe you are still up. That's it. You are getting a spanking." And she does. Through such interactions, the child learns a valuable lesson: obey Mother on trial nineteen.

Third, instead of adapting the child to punishment, have clear standards and consequences for behavior and misbehavior, tell the child what is expected, and apply consequences consistently. If Susie's mother wants Susie to pick up her toys, she should warn Susie, "When the buzzer goes off, pick up your toys and go to bed. If your toys are put away quickly, we'll have time for a story, but if you go slowly, we won't have time."

Fourth, have Susie repeat what she heard.

Fifth, if Susie obeys, praise her. If not, follow through on the consequences. For example, if Susie fails to put away her toys after the buzzer sounds, Susie's mother should make eye contact with Susie, and say, "I'm sorry but we won't have time for a story because you've not put your toys up. Put your toys away now. If you don't, you'll be disobeying, and I'll have to spank you. Now, what do you have to do? And what will happen if you don't do it now?"

If Susie continues to dawdle, her mother will punish her for directly disobeying, following these guidelines.

- Don't punish out of anger. Act before getting worked up.
- Have the child state the reason for punishment. (Don't lecture.)
- Say how much the parent doesn't like to punish the child but state the resolve to punish the child if the child violates the rule.
- Punish the child appropriately for the offense (removing a desired object, denying a privilege, time out, spanking).
- If the child refuses to accept the punishment willingly (e.g., running away from the parent or putting his or her hand behind the bottom if the punishment involves spanking), the parent should tell the child that if the child does not receive the punishment, the child will be punished a second time for disobeying.
- After the punishment, ask the child why he or she was punished.
- Assure the child that the parent loves and cares for the child and forgives the misbehavior.
- State that part of receiving forgiveness is deciding to behave well next time.

6. Develop alternatives to punishment. There are many alternatives to punishment. While parents know this intellectually, they often can't think of creative alternatives when they are locked into problem cycles with their children. You can alert them to some alternatives:

- Allow the child to experience the natural consequences of misbehavior. A natural consequence of failing to put the mother's sewing kit away, even after repeatedly having been instructed to do so, is for mother to deny use of the kit. A natural consequence of not going to bed on time is for the parent to insist that the child go to bed early the next night because a certain amount of sleep is necessary for health.
- The child could be shown how to restore damage done by misbehavior. While parents don't want to teach the child that one can, through effort, make amends for sin, it is appropriate to teach the child that love involves actively trying to restore damaged relationships. For example, a child could work to earn money to pay for a damaged object or scrub walls to remove drawings that had defaced the walls.
- The parent can express strong disapproval of the child's behavior and clearly but calmly express the anger, hurt, or frustration that he or she feels. If the parent always responds with no emotion to a child's misbehavior, the child may not understand that misbehavior can damage relationships and destroy trust as well as have other natural consequences.

Summary

Parents must understand their children at each age and structure their parenting to meet the needs of the children as they grow. Regardless of their age, children need to feel valued, to develop a positive vision for their lives (faith working through love that includes a healthy dependence on God), to develop appropriate strategies for actualizing the vision, to learn discipline, to develop faith, and to have fun.

8

Unified Parenting

God wants husband and wife to help their children become better disciples of Jesus Christ through learning to live in faith working through love. To accomplish this, parents need to work as a unified team.

God's Intentions and Human Imperfections

God gave men and women to each other in marriage, unifying them mystically into one flesh beginning at their marriage and continuing at ever deepening levels as they learn to love each other more over time (Gen. 1:27; 2:23–24). God bade them have children (Gen. 1:28a) and have dominion over the earth as his stewards (Gen. 1:28b).

Sometimes, marriage bonds fracture and the partners grind together in marital conflict even though the break may not be apparent to outsiders. The conflict may be like a hairline stress fracture, causing tenderness but not deeply impairing the marriage. Or the fracture may be profound, erupting in conflict upon little provocation and causing massive pain and distress. Those who counsel broken marriages may wince in empathy. At other times, the marital fracture is compound, with broken bones protruding from wounds, so it is apparent to all that the marriage is ruptured.

Conflict Can Promote Disunity

When a couple or one parent seeks help for a problem in parenting, you hope that the couple is unified in attacking the problem. Sadly, that often isn't true. One parent may ally with the troubled child in a power coalition against the other. Or a parent may focus on the marital power struggle, and problems with children become battlegrounds for superiority, worth, dominance, or power. Help the parents tackle parenting problems in unity.

Stress Can Promote Disunity

Even if there isn't marital conflict, stress can build until a parent's nerves feel as if there is sand in his or her bathing suit—leaving private parts chafed, raw, and frazzled. Little things irritate. Frustrations grate. Disappointments plunge the person into the pit. Elations are barely enjoyed. Stressed-out parents are self-focused parents, and children usually bear the brunt of the parents' stress.

Family History Can Promote Disunity

Some parents simply can't get together on parenting. They each act out separate parent scripts like their parents before them, with little reflection about their joint priorities. Again, children suffer.

Marital Conflict and Adjustment in Children

Marital Conflict Is Related to Children's Adjustment Problems

Substantial research has associated marital conflict with the presence of adjustment problems in children of all ages (Fincham, Grych & Osborne 1994). Adjustment problems might include guilt, depression, aggressiveness, sibling fighting, enmeshment in parents' problems, and anxieties.

Not all marital conflict leads children to have problems. Children can learn how to resolve conflict amicably by watching their parents discuss and resolve their differences if parents practice good conflict-resolution skills. You may need to help parents develop such skills.

Some Marital Conflict May Produce Problems in Children

However, certain types of marital conflict are often associated with children developing problems (Fincham 1994; Fincham, Grych & Osborne 1994; Rutter 1994). Marital conflict that is frequent, intense, poorly resolved or unresolved, child-related, physically aggressive, or verbally aggressive and hostile is most likely to be associated with childhood problems.

Even if conflict has all the worst characteristics, though, not every child will develop problems. One sibling may have problems while another may not. Children who are emotionally reactive, sensitive, and don't soothe themselves well are prone to develop adjustment problems when the parents are in conflict. Also, children who think that they are the cause of the parental conflict—perhaps due to parents who disagree in front of their children over child discipline or other child-related topics—tend to blame themselves, suffer lowered self-esteem, depression, and guilt. Children who feel threatened by conflict—perhaps fearing divorce, abandonment, aggression, or blame by the parents—often act aggressively toward children and adults.

Girls tend to appraise themselves to be the cause of their parents' problems more often than do boys, while boys tend to appraise their parent-child relationship as threatened by their parents' conflict more often than do girls. Still, gender of the child doesn't account for all differences in the ways children react to parental conflict (Cummings, Davies & Simpson 1994; Fincham, Grych & Osborne 1994).

Divorce—The Ultimate Parenting Disunity

Divorce is often the result of intense marital conflict. Divorce ends the legal marriage but often does not end conflict (Cherlin, Furstenberg, Chase-Lansdale, Kierman, Robins, Morrison & Teitler 1991). Divorce can have traumatic effects on children extending as many as ten years after the divorce (Emery 1988; Wallerstein & Blakeslee 1991).

The Bottom Line

The research on parental disunity, whether through hurtful conflict within marriage or highly conflictual divorce, is clear. It is generally better for parents and children to work hard to resolve conflict than to assume that the negative effects of the conflict will end simply because the couple divorces. In some cases—such as where there is physical violence between partners, child abuse, or child sexual abuse—separation and counseling are recommended, but those are the exceptions.

Help Parents Who Aren't Unified Work Together in Parenting

Break Up Coalitions

Sometimes lack of unity between partners occurs because a coalition exists between one parent and a troubled child. In most coalitions one parent is overinvolved and exasperated with the child and the other parent is underinvolved and detached. Jay Haley (1987), noted family therapist, says that a troubled child can exert more control in the family than either parent only if the child is standing on a parent's shoulders.

In a family whose counseling I supervised several years ago, the mother had a girl (then eight years old) by a previous husband. Neither mother nor new husband could make the eight-year-old girl obey. A destructive cycle was at work. The mother would invite the stepfather to discipline the girl. He would yell and scold. The mother would then criticize his "barbaric" behavior, so he would withdraw. The mother would try to discipline the child, who wouldn't obey. Exasperated, the mother would invite the stepfather to discipline the girl. He would yell and scold. The cycle continued, frustrating both parents and leaving a disobedient girl who continually was scolded, yelled at, and criticized. No one was happy.

In treating the family, our first step was to break up the coalition between the mother and daughter. As long as the coalition continued, the cycle was set in stone. We suggested that the father help the child keep a neater room and do better at school. A time was set aside each night for the stepfather and daughter to talk, and we helped the father talk to his stepdaughter without criticizing and yelling. Their relationship improved while the mother struggled not to interfere.

We knew that the mother and daughter would always be closer than would the stepfather and daughter, but we wanted to allow the coalition between daughter and mother to cool off. After a few weeks, the stepfather could discipline his stepdaughter better than previously, and the mother and stepfather could discipline the child together.

In weakening a parent-child coalition, break up habitual patterns that keep the family in bondage. That will allow the family to consider more constructive solutions.

Deal with Marital Differences apart from Parenting

When parents argue heatedly, violently, or hurtfully in front of their children, children may (1) feel threatened that the marriage will end and the children will be abandoned, (2) feel that they are to blame for their parents' discord (especially if parents' disagreements involve child rearing), and (3) copy the parents' verbal aggression. Coach parents not to argue heatedly in front of children. If an argument breaks out in front of a child, have parents tell the child later that the child wasn't to blame and that the parents' disagreement has been resolved (Fincham 1994). If conflict between parents is long-standing and bitter, suggest marital counseling.

If you conduct the marriage counseling, separate it from counseling for parenting problems. For example, suppose you are counseling the Thayers because their son is aggressive toward other children. Despite his parents' and second-grade teacher's efforts, he continues to provoke fights at school and at home with his siblings. Both partners have attended two sessions about their parenting problems. By that time, you realize that the Thayers have serious marital conflict. Their poisonous arguments spew venom during counseling, at church, and at a Bible study they attend. Approach them this way. Suggest that their conflict might be contributing to their son's aggressive behavior. Suggest that you take a break from the remaining three sessions aimed at solving their parenting troubles and recommend that you meet with them for five sessions to address their marital conflict. If they agree, use the related approach that promotes faith working through love during marriage counseling (see *Marriage Conflicts* coauthored by Ev and Douglas McMurry [1994]—also in the Strategic Pastoral Counseling series).

If the Thayers don't want to attend marriage counseling with you, or if you believe that their problems are too severe for you to counsel them effectively, then refer them to counseling with a professional Christian counselor (if one is available) and recess your counseling for their parenting problems until the marital conflicts have been addressed. Generally, it is not a good idea for a couple to see two counselors simultaneously. They may perceive the counsel they receive as contradictory because the goals of marital and parenting counseling may be different. Even if you are counseling the couple for both marital and parenting concerns, don't do both at the same time. Goals become easily confused and the couple may lose focus.

When Marital Conflicts Can't Be Resolved

Even if marital conflicts can't be resolved, you can still help the couple parent better. Find things that the parents can agree on. Most couples have common goals for their families. Investigate whether couples can agree on the following:

- promoting faith and spiritual development in the child
- employing Christian parenting principles (faith working through love)
- dealing with the parents' own stresses
- not criticizing each other in front of the children (preferably never criticizing each other)
- showing the child love and affection
- having positive experiences as a family—those that the whole family find pleasant (If parents can avoid power struggles in deciding what the family would consider pleasant, that can teach children to sacrifice on behalf of others.)

If parents can agree on common goals, have them work toward those goals. Often, the parents will become more cooperative, and conflict will lessen.

Promote Unity by Reducing Parents' Stress

Effects of Stress

Forehand, Wells, McMahon, Griest, and Rogers (1982) have
found that when under high stress, parents are more bothered by
their children's misbehavior than they normally are. Thus, if parents can reduce their stress, they'll automatically reduce (but not
necessarily eliminate) parenting problems. Reducing stress is not
easy. Under high stress parents are more bothered by their own
problems and may also lose their unity as a couple.

The Prison of Stress

Our modern world is characterized by rapid change and too
much to do in too little time. We are prisoners of stress. Some prisons restrict us as surely as a maximum security prison with tall
walls, strong bars, armed guards, and patrolling dogs. For example, restrictive prisons might include overcommitment, criticism
of others, competing with the Joneses, anxieties, fear of others,
fear of failure, past hurts, and lack of forgiveness. Other prisons
sweep us along like the prison ship in *Ben Hur*, where a slave ham-
mers out an invariant cadence for the prisoners to match with
strong rowing. These prisons include ambition, striving for success, desperately seeking approval, vainly pursuing love, longing
for acceptance from a parent who won't or can't give it, and working for perfection.

Sometimes prisons are squalid and dank, like a small cell during
the Spanish Inquisition. At other times prisons are luxurious, like
the imprisonment of the royal family at the end of Czarist Russia.
Either way, prisons control and stress us.

Some prisons are especially connected with the child-rearing
years. Overidentification with the child, in which a parent seeks to
achieve his or her own dreams through squashing the child into a
narrow mold, can imprison parent and child. Submitting to one's
own childhood difficulties by repeating patterns or rigidly swinging to the opposite extreme can imprison and drive us in ways we
can't seem to refuse. Inability to control frustration, anger, depression, or anxieties can cause enormous stress and leave parents feel-

ing out of control and disheartened. Also stressful is having no time for taking care of one's mental and physical health.

Jailbreak

Parents may try to burst free of stress by their own efforts or by enlisting counselors, friends, or self-help groups. Parents may achieve release through their own efforts, but not freedom. Their own efforts are a jailbreak. Even if successful, parents are always harried, harassed, and unfulfilled. They are always dodging the law of love.

True Freedom

Only Jesus can set parents truly free. "The Spirit of the Lord is on me," quoted Jesus at the beginning of his ministry, "to proclaim freedom for the prisoners . . . to release the oppressed" (Luke 4:18, 19a). John says of Jesus, "So, if the Son sets you free, you will be free indeed" (John 8:36). Paul concurs: "Now the Lord is the Spirit, and where the Spirit of the Lord is, there is freedom" (2 Cor. 3:17).

The Lord Jesus and the leaders of Christianity agree. By turning to Jesus, people find real freedom. Encourage the parents who seek your help for release from stress to look to the real source of freedom.

Help Parents Unify in Parenting by Faith Working through Love

If counseling works well, parents unify on a strategy for parenting—applying the discipleship principle of faith working through love. Several practical guidelines can help parents think about the strategy as they make their momentary decision about how to react to their child. We have compiled some of these practical principles in Table 8–1.

Work throughout counseling to convey this strategy to parents and to have them unify to put the message into practice in their family. Photocopy the guidelines given in Table 8–1 and have parents reflect on those guidelines throughout counseling

Table 8–1
Principles of Parenting by
Faith Working through Love

Parenting by Faith
- faith trusts in something beyond yourself (Jesus)
- faith inspires hope in your child
- faith looks for the positive in your child, your partner, and the situation

Parenting Requires Work
- work is not expecting that faith and love will simply happen; rather, faith and love require constant effort
- work can be and should be fun
- work combines firm control with constant emotional support
- work is thinking ahead about what might happen and how to prevent the bad and promote the good; that requires effort
- work is modeling the behaviors you want the child to imitate

Parenting in Love
- *love values the child*
  - love tells and shows your child that you love him or her regardless of what happens
  - love listens to understand (not to prove a point)
  - love encourages the child by
    * building up the child publicly and privately
    * allowing the child to have responsibilities
    * recognizing children's areas of expertise
    * respecting your child's individuality
    * allowing choices
  - love rewards good behavior with appropriate rewards (tangible for young children moving to social recognition, praise, and approval for older children)
  - love acts consistently
  - love ignores minor misbehaviors that aren't serious
  - love punishes effectively when punishment is necessary—punish privately, respect the child's integrity
- *love doesn't devalue the child*
  - love never puts down the child (even in humor)
  - love doesn't talk negatively about the child
  - love doesn't expect misbehavior

9

Positive Parenting

If you prospect for gold in the same empty places you always have, you'll find no gold. Parents often seek the gold of harmonious parenting in the played-out mines of negative cycles.

Negative Cycles of Conflict within the Family

Argumentative, discordant relationships between spouses or between parents and children spiral into negative cycles that affect the child's faith, work, and love.

Discordant relations between parents affect the child's *faith*. When parents conflict, the child loses faith that he or she has a stable, nurturing base. Child developmentalists call this loss of secure attachment (Bowlby 1969), which can lead to insecure avoidance or anxious resistance.

Discordant relations between parents also affect the child's *work* or effort to obtain acceptance. A child may not seek support within the family because he or she doubts that the family can provide acceptance. Instead, the child within a conflictual family tends to pick peers who also have problems and eventually chooses a spouse who has problems from whom he or she tries to obtain acceptance and nurture.

Discordant relations between parents also affect the *love* experienced by the child. When parents repeatedly fail to value the child or actively devalue the child, not surprisingly the child doesn't feel valuable, which affects most aspects of the child's life. In addition, the child learns how to relate to others by watching how the parents relate to each other and to the children. If the child observes the parents relating to others through conflict, anger, hostility, hurtfulness, and manipulation, then the child learns those strategies.

Each of these reactions of the child—insecure attachments, selection of troubled peers (and eventually a troubled spouse), poor self-esteem, and poor interpersonal behavior—feeds back to the parents. The parents see the child's troubled behavior, and the parents become more troubled themselves. A feedback loop occurs in which negative feeds negative.

Negative Cycles in Child Discipline

A similar negative cycle can develop in child discipline. Whenever we encounter blocks to our goals, we rarely give in. Instead, we try harder to remove the block. The more the block resists us, the more we struggle to make it succumb. If, after exerting strong effort, we still can't remove the block, we may become focused on removing the block, almost obsessed with it.

Children's problems can block parental goals. Most parents want their children to have as few problems as possible. When a child won't obey, pick up her room, make acceptable grades in school, make new friends, or get over a rejection, parents try to help. Usually, parents are excellent helps to their children because the parents have gone through similar struggles and bring the wisdom of experience to bear on the child's problem. But sometimes, the parents' advice doesn't help or children reject parents' guidance.

Parents respond predictably. They may have tried nagging, badgering, putting down, or other devaluing strategies to produce change. If those fail, they try harder, louder, and sometimes nastier—until either the problem is solved or the parent is completely focused on the problem. In frustration the parent becomes locked into thinking that if he or she tries harder then the problem will disappear. Both parent and child repeat the same failures, the same frustrations, and keep trying the same destructive solutions, each getting louder. They are caught in a negative cycle.

Teaching as a Negative Cycle

Parents can get into a pattern of continually teaching their children to do things better. Eager to help their child, parents can forget that part of teaching is complimenting the child for good behavior. Without sincere compliments, parents are ensnared in a "negative teaching trap." Good teaching must balance compliments and correction.

The Solution to Negative Cycles

Gordius, legendary king of Phrygia, tied a complicated knot. He said that whoever could untie the Gordian knot was destined to rule Asia. All who tried failed, until Alexander the Great of Macedonia. At first, he fruitlessly tried to find a starting point. Then he drew his sword and whacked the knot in half, freeing multiple ends to unravel. The rest is history.

Have parents break free of a negative cycle by trying something different, not trying the same things harder and louder. Things that make a difference are positive faith, positive work, and positive love.

Positive Faith

Parenting based on faith working through love is characterized by positive faith. Positive faith is belief in the God of the Bible and his saving work through Jesus' death and resurrection and the giving of the Holy Spirit. Positive faith is trusting God, even when we don't understand him or his actions. Like Job, we can confidently say, "Though he slay me, yet will I hope in him" (Job 13:15a).

Positive faith is realistic. It doesn't promise perfection on earth. It promises redemption. Parents who grasp this fact of Christian faith are freed to make mistakes in the confident knowledge that Jesus redeems his own. That doesn't provide a license for intentionally sinning or for sloppy parenting, but it provides assurance that if parents try to glorify God through parenting and they make mistakes or bad decisions, then God will hear their confessions and will forgive (and often redeem) their mistakes.

Positive faith looks for the good in life; it is optimistic. According to psychologist Martin Seligman (1991), in *Learned Optimism*, optimistic people are healthier beginning in their midforties, have fewer bouts of depression, and achieve more of their goals than do pessimistic people.

Not only does positive faith prevent problems, but it also helps people get over psychological problems. Chang (1994) found that counselees who talked about their positive hopes and expectations and their successes in life were more likely to change in counseling than were people who talked about more negative things. Furthermore, counselees were more likely to change and to maintain their changes if the counselor was encouraging, supportive, and positive. This suggests that during counseling, you not only should be positive yourself but should also encourage your parishioners to discuss the positive aspects of their lives as well as the things that are going wrong. That is not always easy when people are besieged with unsolved problems and frustrations with their children.

Positive Work

As problems build, people adapt to negative experiences. Like getting into a too-hot bath that we soon get used to, when family life is negative, we soon adapt to that. *It's normal*, we think. But it isn't normal.

In Eleanor Porter's (1913) *Pollyanna*, an orphan comes to live in a town full of bitterness and strife. Through relying on Scripture, Pollyanna, by playing the "glad game," changes people's outlook to one that trusts God. In the glad game, people try to find the positive in a situation. It isn't easy. It requires effort and concentration. But it works.

Charles Sheldon (1985), in his classic book, *In His Steps*, addresses a similar theme. In Sheldon's town, people pledge to make every decision the way they believe Jesus would make the decision. That requires self-sacrifice and dedication, but as a result, the town is transformed.

Those works of fiction capture a truth and portray it in a way that is easily remembered and understood. Through effort, faith, and love, amazing transformations from negative to positive are possible.

In family therapy, one of the newest popular therapies is a revolutionary approach to family problems. *Clues: Investigating Solutions in Brief Therapy*, by Steve deShazer (1988), suggests that people wallow in negative emotional traps because they focus on their problems. Even well-meaning therapies often focus people on their problems. DeShazer's solution-focused therapy, however, maintains that people often already know how to solve their own problems. Usually, things worked better once, but people stopped doing what worked. As problems mounted, people got even further from what once worked. DeShazer urges people to find and reemploy previous solutions. That isn't easy. It often requires great effort for families to examine their pasts and recapture solutions. DeShazer reports many successes through helping people focus more positively.

Some adults may have been reared in hurtful families, may not know good solutions, and may never have functioned according to God's plan. Help them find new, positive, godly solutions, not reemploy faulty patterns.

Research on marital therapy by John Gottman (1993a, 1993b), which we described earlier, suggests that happy marriages have at least five positive interactions for every negative interaction. We believe this to be true of parenting as well. Positive interactions won't happen without work. Having fun with one's spouse or children takes effort, but so does trying to pick up the pieces after negative interactions. The difference—it's positive, not negative work.

Positive work is more motivating than negative work is. When parents consult you, they generally anticipate the parenting equivalent of visiting the dentist for a mouthful of root canals. Family life isn't fun. It's no wonder that they are reluctant to try new behaviors.

Restore their excitement. Almost all parents were ecstatic when their first child was born. They whipped out snapshots at the slightest excuse, showed home videos to whomever was handy, and talked about their child to strangers they met in the supermarket. How can they regain that enthusiasm? Ask them. What did they previously do as a family that was fun? Set them to puzzling how to regain the solutions. Stimulate them to positive work.

Positive Love

Ask Parents to Find Their Sweet Fragrance

Pushing never draws anyone closer.

A honey bee is drawn to a flower because of the nectar it can give. Ask parents to speculate about what kind of nectar they can give their children. What do they have, or what can they cultivate, that the child can see in them and want to have?

Children are drawn to:

- valuing love
- verbal and physical displays of affection
- stimulating thought
- laughter and play
- a sense of wonder
- personal communication
- adults who show wisdom and humility

How can parents cultivate those sources of interpersonal nectar? And how can parents show their children, without pretension, that the parent has those qualities, thus sending off a sweet fragrance that can be sensed?

Positive Love through Forgiveness

In troubled families, both parents and children have hurt each other. Parents must not harbor unforgiveness. Nor can they wait until their children confess their transgression and seek forgiveness. After all, *parents* are the family's adults, not children. *Parents* must forgive first.

In homes where child problems are severe, parents may feel betrayed, devalued, unappreciated, and impotent to have any positive effect on their children. Forgiveness is even more important in those homes.

Positive love means being eager to forgive. Sergeant Jacob de-Shazer—no relation to the family therapist mentioned earlier—was captured by Japan in World War II (Kennedy & Newcombe 1994; Prange, Goldstein & Dillon 1990). In a prison camp, he was mistreated, confined to a small cell, and abused by the guards. Only his growing hatred of the guards kept him from despair. His hatred became a river, an ocean wave, a tidal wave.

A Bible was circulated within the prison camp, and deShazer read it—not because he was a Christian but because he wanted to rebel against camp rules. To deShazer's surprise, that Bible led him to Jesus, who became deShazer's Savior. Even so, deShazer's bitterness didn't disappear. One day he read Luke 23:34a, in which Jesus said, "Father forgive them, for they know not what they do." Those words set deShazer free from bitterness, hatred, retaliation. His tidal wave of rage became a trickle.

Soon, his freedom from hatred was tested. A guard slammed the cell door maliciously on deShazer's bare foot, then stomped the foot. DeShazer didn't respond with the usual hatred. Instead, he thought of Jesus' words, "Love your enemies." Seeing deShazer's response, the guard's attitude eventually changed. Forgiveness' freedom from hatred and bitterness had not only set the captive deShazer free, it had set his captor free, too!

At the end of the war, deShazer was repatriated to the United States. You'd think he would be glad to be finished with the Japanese. Instead, he returned to Japan as a missionary, where he served for years. His tidal wave of rage had become a wellspring of living water for others.

DeShazer's story of love and forgiveness during war was printed into a tract, which was widely distributed throughout postwar Japan. Captain Mitsuo Fuchida, the man who had led the air attack on Pearl Harbor on December 7, 1941, which started U.S. involvement in the war, was discouraged and defeated. One day, he received deShazer's tract in the street.

Fuchida read it, sought missionaries and other Christians, and became a converted Christian. He preached throughout Japan and eventually in the United States. In fact, he spoke at a ceremony commemorating the twenty-fifth anniversary of the attack on Pearl Harbor. With him, he brought a gift for each survivor who attended the ceremony: a Bible inscribed with Luke 23:34a: "Father, forgive them for they know not what they do."

Jesus freed Sergeant Jacob deShazer from hatred and set him on the path of forgiveness. He freed Captain Mitsuo Fuchida from defeat, depression, and discouragement and set him also on the path of forgiveness. If Jesus can work such transformations in the midst of the horrors of war and prison camps, then he can heal parents of the hurts they have received at their children's usually unwitting hands. This will free the parents to show positive love. "Father, help us forgive them, even if they know in part what they do."

Positive Love through Listening

One way to value the child is through listening carefully to the child. Listening involves giving undivided attention. For instance, when Christen—our oldest, now 18—was two years old, I was grading papers when she came into my room to talk. I did what most parents do when they are busy. I continued to work while I pretended to listen to her—all the while sending nonverbal messages that, "Daddy's busy." I also learned what most parents learn: nonverbal messages make as much of an impression on a two-year-old as does speaking Portuguese. Eventually, I got the message. Putting down my papers, I patted the bed beside me and sat attentively as Christen told me something. It took about three minutes. On the way out of the room she said, "Daddy, you like talking to me, don't you?" I do enjoy talking with my children. But sometimes it helps to be reminded.

Through giving Christen a few minutes of undivided attention, I showed Christen that I valued her. If I had continued nonverbally to say, "Go away; I'm busy," both she and I would have left frustrated, and it might have taken ten times as long.

Explaining the Negatives Positively

At times, every parent must deny his or her child some request. Middle-schooler Susie says, "I want to watch MTV tonight. The Green Punk Wave Hairpiece is on Stony Stone's Show at eight o'clock. Everybody's watching it. Can I, Mama?"

Many snappy retorts spring nimbly and instantly to parental minds such as, "Not everyone is watching it—you're not." Or "Get used to disappointment." Or (my personal favorite), "Television will rot your brain." Parents probably inherited such responses from their parents, or, if not genetic, at least their parents taught such clever answers.

If parents respond with a flip or sarcastic "No," they may devalue the child. They don't mean to, but a glib "No" says to the child that he or she is wrong (and the parent is right, and also more powerful, and P.S. never listens). The child thinks, *Mom doesn't trust me. She never lets me do what the other kids do. She wants me to grow up with no friends. She wants me to be an adult and won't let me enjoy my childhood.*

This is not to say that parents should give in if they believe an activity that the child wants to do might be harmful. To the contrary, protecting their children's welfare is an important parental task. However, even in refusing the request, the mother can still value her teenager.

First, the mother must understand why her daughter wants to do the behavior—not the specific action but the big picture. Susie is struggling with gaining acceptance from her peers, and she believes that watching the show will bond her to her peer group. Adolescent relationships are often volatile. Not being "in" in even a small way might trigger a rejection.

Second, the mother must ask, *How can I show Susie that I value her?* "Missing the show would be bad, huh?" she asks.

"Yeah, everybody's watching it."

"And you want to be able to talk about it to your friends?"

"Uh-huh."

"I think that those shows on MTV aren't good for you, but I know that it's important to be able to talk about current things with your friends. Is there any way that you can keep up with current things without watching MTV?"

"Well, maybe if I could listen to Power 104's Week in Review on Saturday night, I'd know the hot songs."

"That would be a good solution."

In this case, Susie's mother identified the need behind the request and helped Susie see that there are many ways to meet needs. This is usually the case. Getting locked into an argument about whether one way of behaving is allowable leads to many negative interactions. Identifying the needs leads to more positive solutions.

Promoting Positive Parenting

Throughout this chapter, we have suggested that you promote positive parenting through taking a positive approach to faith, work, and love. When parents are locked into negative patterns, help them focus on the positive, which will open healthier interactions and lead to forgiveness and healing.

Part 3

Strategic Pastoral Counseling of Parents

10

Encounter Stage

As you begin to counsel a person, you must encounter him or her personally—whether you've know the person for years or minutes. Without such personal encounter, the best advice falls on deaf ears. Encounter involves three tasks: structuring counseling so that everyone knows what to expect, joining the parent to solve the problem he or she presents, and assessing the problem and what to do about it.

Structuring

Be Clear about Who You Are Trying to Help

When parents seek your help for problems with their child, it is easy to get confused about who you're trying to help. You can't help the child directly. You can only help the parents. Parents have sought your help, are listening to your counsel, and will change their behavior. They may *want* you to "fix" their child or to show them how to "fix" their child, but you can only help the person you are looking at—the parent.

Even if you could, you wouldn't want to ride in on a white horse and solve the child's difficulty. You want to help parents solve their problems. In five sessions, you'll be out of the picture, but they'll be parenting for years. If you solve their child's problem, they'll be back to see you the next time their child has a problem. And the next. It may feel good to be needed, but that isn't your goal. You want to promote a mature dependence on God, not on you.

Agree on Goals

In five sessions, goals must be modest. At times, God works miraculously, transforming people's lives. If that happens in counseling, great. Give God the glory. Usually, though, achievements will be modest.

In five sessions, try to make a small but fundamental change in the parent's life that will set him or her on a new path. Counseling is a fork in the trail. At any trail junction, the traveler has a choice of paths. Often, the paths diverge only slightly at first, but they may direct the traveler to completely different destinations.

Above all, help the parent think of every decision in terms of promoting faith working through love. Counseling will succeed to the extent that you can get parents to pause at decision points and ask, "How can I promote more faith?" or "How can I inspire my child to greater positive effort?" or "How can I value my child more and help my child value others more?" If you help the parent solve the presenting problem, wonderful. But if you help the parent see his or her task as building a child into a more effective disciple of Jesus or as acting as a better disciple of Christ within his or her own family, then you have achieved true success. Then, many presenting problems will disappear and many future problems will never materialize.

Agree on the Number of Sessions and What You Expect Will Occur

Most people enter pastoral counseling without understanding what will happen. Their ideas are based on television, novels, other counseling experience, or even previous counseling with you. Counseling will progress more smoothly if you make your expectations clear at the start and if the parent agrees with you about what will occur. Understanding that you will meet together for no more than five sessions will focus the parent's efforts.

After beginning with a few pleasantries, say,

Before we start, let's understand what might happen in counseling. I assume that you want to accomplish as much as you can in as little time as possible. I've found that most people can change a lot within a month or so. I know that we can't take care of all your concerns in a month, but you can make the crucial changes in only five sessions. If difficult problems still exist after five meetings, you should seek help from someone who has more expertise than I. What do you think?

Don't talk much. Give the person a chance to react. You'll quickly see whether the person had a different expectation about counseling. Be prepared to address common reactions such as:

- "I'm not sure that our problems can be handled so quickly." People have tried, sometimes for years, to deal with a difficulty. The idea that something can be done in a mere five weeks threatens their competence, and they are skeptical. Say, "I understand that your problem is serious and that you have tried many solutions that haven't worked. I can't solve your problem either, but I hope to set you on a different path that will help you eliminate the problem as you practice what you learn."
- "I didn't think it would take that long." Some people have a "magic-bullet" theory. They believe that you'll be able to meet with them once—twice tops—and fire the magic bullet that will slay the problem. Say, "It will be hard work, but you'll benefit by your effort."
- "Do we have to be this structured?" Some people expect counseling to be free-wheeling and unfocused. Say, "We want to help you as effectively and efficiently as possible. Being structured is the most respectful of your time and effort."
- "What if we're making progress but are not done after five sessions?" Say, "Let's wait and see. Generally, if we're going to make progress, it will be within five sessions. You'll probably never feel 'completely done.' Parenting problems will always spring up, but by five sessions, you should have a better idea how to deal with those."

Agree on the Parent's Responsibilities

Counseling is a two-way street. Both you and the parents have responsibilities. Merely talking about what parents can do differently will never solve their problems. They must apply at home what they learn in counseling. Without parents' work at practicing faith and love at home, counseling is worse than worthless, but if parents try to make changes at home—even if the changes don't work—they still learn about parenting. Parents' responsibilities are as follows:

- Honestly disclosing what's going on.
- Open-mindedly listening to what you say.
- Thinking about what occurred during counseling.
- Reading the book that accompanies this book (*Value Your Children*) and employing its suggestions.
- Being willing to change their parenting between sessions.
- Thinking about what is going on at home.
- Committing to pray for their children, spouse, and counseling.

Joining

Don't Let Other Roles Interfere

When you counsel someone in your congregation, you are dealing with a situation that professional mental health counselors avoid as an ethical dilemma. It's called dual roles. Dual roles contaminate professional counseling, which is a series of strongly bounded professional contacts with clearly prescribed behavior for counselor and client. Dual roles create ethical problems because counseling offers potential for counselors to influence their clients, who are vulnerable, in ways that help the counselor but are not in the primary welfare of the client.

With pastoral counseling, though, you are necessarily in dual roles with members of your congregation. Instead of looking at your other roles as a danger in counseling, look at counseling as an important part of your larger commitment to pastoral care for the person. Pastoral care might involve promoting their Christian education through Sunday school, sermons, or small groups, visiting your parishioners during a physical, relationship, or spiritual crisis, praying for them, and providing moral and spiritual leadership for them.

As with all pastoral care, though, there is always the possibility that your own interests may intrude on your calling as a pastor. As a result of the fall, people are sinful and imperfect—even pastors, as you know well. Your darker motives can be activated when you are in a variety of roles.

- You can become overconcerned with your own importance. Being respected as pastor can lead you to expect that others will respect you in all things. If they don't, you can be tempted to use counseling to gain respect.
- You can use other pastoral roles—such as preaching at the counselee—in counseling, even though they are not helpful.
- You can allow friendship to interfere with counseling. This is especially dangerous when you counsel a couple about parenting. You might be a stronger friend to one partner than to the other, which might make you support that person more in a conflict.
- If you are counseling a powerful lay leader or one who has the power to influence your salary, duties, or favorite projects, you might be reluctant to confront.

People whom you counsel will react to you as pastor, not just as counselor. For example:

- They might expect the forthright advice that is typical of sermons but not of counseling.
- They might censor what they tell you because they are ashamed or think that you wouldn't want to hear about their failings.
- They might play on their friendship with you, especially if a power struggle exists between spouses.
- If you are often confrontive in sermons, they may expect the same in counseling; if you are usually warm and supportive in sermons and social interactions, they may expect that you won't confront them in counseling.

You can't possibly directly address all of the role expectations that you or the people you counsel hold. Rather, be aware of the possibilities that other roles can contaminate your counseling. Get support from another pastor or trusted confidant whom you can consult in confidence when difficulties arise in counseling. Don't consult a lay person in your congregation. If you reveal information about another member of the congregation, you might be thought to be gossiping. Don't consult your spouse. When problems happen, you usually don't need someone who will support you as much as you need someone who can offer a detached opinion about what you should do. That may require the person to give you some hard-to-take advice. Don't place your spouse in that position.

Make an Emotional Connection

Emotion energizes you and the people you help. Make an emotional connection if you want to help effectively.

Connect emotionally through listening actively. Connect emotionally through empathic listening (Miller, Wackman, Nunnally & Miller 1988).

- Make following comments (like "Um-hum," or "I see") that indicate you are tracking the parent's story.
- Summarize the parent's emotional experience or actions briefly (like "You're angry," or "So, you threw the toys") to show that you picked up the key aspect of a parent's experience.
- Invite the parent to continue with the story (like "Tell me more," or "What happened then?").
- Suggest detailed summaries through paraphrasing, digesting an experience into a brief paragraph, and checking out whether the summary is accurate (like "Let's see if I understand. You got furious with Tim and threw the toys. That broke the television, and you felt guilty for losing your temper, ashamed that you had failed in self-control, and depressed over your inability to control your anger. Is that right?").

These listening techniques serve many purposes. They focus your attention, demonstrate to the parent that you understand his or her experience accurately, and show the parent that you care and are concentrating on understanding him or her. But primarily, actively listening creates an emotional bond between you and the parent in two ways. It shows the parent that you care for him or her, and it shows *you* that you care for the parent. By listening actively, you'll actually feel more empathy. You need to care to be an effective helper. The concept of a detached therapist is not God's plan. Think about how Christ helped. He cared.

Connect emotionally through praying for the parent. Praying for those you counsel creates both a spiritual and emotional bond between you. More importantly, it invites God's intervention. Counseling sessions will usually begin with prayer—especially after the first session. At the beginning of the first session, you may not know enough about the person and his or her problem to pray with discernment. Beyond the first session, begin with prayer that invites Jesus to guide and empower counseling and pray for the parent's specific needs.

Pray during the session. Silent arrow prayers, aimed at specific targets that arise during conversation, keep you focused on God as the true counselor. Brief prayers (aloud) at times of perplexity demonstrate to the parent that you seek God's wisdom when you are confused (and help the parent see the benefits in doing so). Prayer at the close of each session sends the parent away from counseling with the knowledge that God is with him or her in the pursuit of whatever homework the parent will attempt between sessions. Prayer binds pastor and parent together emotionally and spiritually as a team with God as the captain.

Motivate the Person to Faith, Work, and Love

Psychologists who study motivations tell us that there are two fundamental types of motivations. Internal drives usually push people toward satisfying a need (such as a need for food, water, air, sex, safety, security, meaning, love, self-esteem, the esteem of others, beauty, justice, and truth). External incentives stimulate people to pursue rewards or avoid punishments—such as to pursue happiness or avoid painful conflict in the family. You can highlight both needs and incentives to motivate parents to work for change.

Need. People need the Lord. Pascal called it the "God-shaped vacuum" within the human heart. By helping parents remain aware of that need and of how Jesus fills it, you can help motivate them to live according to God's pattern for discipleship and thus "spur one another on toward love and good deeds" (Heb. 10:24).

Incentive. Following God's pattern for discipleship is rewarding. It works. Jonathan, now 16, went on a youth retreat this past weekend. After his return, he said, "On this retreat, I got along better with Stewart [not his real name] than ever before."

"How'd that happen?" I asked.

"Whenever he talked, I listened, and I asked him about himself and about what he was interested in. After we'd talked, he didn't bug me."

"So if you valued Stewart, he responded like something valuable."

"Yeah. It was great."

Help parents value their children. They'll be rewarded. The children will act as if they are more valuable.

Assessing

Without a good assessment, counseling probably won't be effective. Under ideal conditions, you might want to give personality tests, interview the person several times, ask others what their observations of the problem have been, bring both of the parents (and perhaps others involved in the problem) in to talk about the problem, visit the home or school, where most of the problem is occurring, and observe what is happening. To conduct such a thorough assessment, of course, you would need to resign the pastorate because you'd be spending all of your time assessing this one problem.

Instead, we have boiled down the assessment to ten questions that you should ask the parent. As you listen to the parent's answers, keep a mental accounting of not only his or her answer but also of your impressions, which may differ from the person's perceptions. We have summarized the ten questions in Table 10–1. Photocopy and use this table during counseling.

Table 10–1
Ten Questions to Ask in the Early Sessions to Assess the Dark Problems

***D**escribe the Duration and Distress*

1. What is going on that you are having trouble handling as a parent?
2. How long has this been going on?
3. How much does this problem bother you?

***A**ffect Other Areas*

4. Other than this problem, how are things going with your parenting?
5. What else is happening in your lives or in your family that might be making this problem hard to solve?

***R**esponses: Recapture Solutions*

6. How are you dealing with the problem now and what have you tried?
7. What resources do you have to help you deal with this difficulty?
8. What have you done before when things were going better in the family?
9. What could you do to recapture any of those better times?

***K**ingship of Jesus*

10. Where do you see God in all this, and how can you let him be more involved?

What Is Going on That You Are Having Trouble Handling as a Parent?

Have the parent describe the problem as he or she sees it. Don't ask a specific question, which will guide the parent's answer. Notice how we phrased this question. It implies that counseling will help the parent, not fix the child.

How Long Has This Been Going On?

You need to know the duration and severity of the problem. Here you're asking about the duration of the problem. Problems that have existed for a long time are likely to be more resistant to change. Avoid simplistic suggestions, especially with long-existing problems.

How Much Does This Problem Bother You?

People need to talk about their feelings. They will usually be frustrated, angry, depressed, and anxious. Their feelings may be so strong that their problem solving is inhibited or may be just strong enough to motivate them to work hard at solving the difficulty.

Watch their nonverbal behavior to get a sense of how much the problems bother the parents, but also ask for their perceptions. Some people normally react strongly. Every little crisis elicits strong emotion. If you see strong emotion, you might conclude that they are very upset, but to them this is a normal little crisis. Other people hardly ever react emotionally. You might interpret a small show of anger as no big deal, but the person may feel almost out of control.

Other Than This Problem, How Are Things Going with Your Parenting?

Problems can be localized or general. One mother may simply have difficulty stopping one child from writing on the walls. Another mother might have a child who disobeys constantly and writing on the walls is one instance; however, she might have no problems with her other two sons. A third mother might have an entire household of children who disobey and one child's writing on the walls was merely the trigger that brought her to counseling. How you deal with each problem differs.

What Else Is Happening in Your Lives or in Your Family That Might Be Making This Problem Hard to Solve?

Marital problems. Many factors can complicate solving the parenting problem and helping the parent grow spiritually. Marital disputes often occur in tandem with child problems. In some families, the children's problems seem to be a direct result of the marital tensions, but in other families the marital tensions may be a product of the parents' inability to solve the children's problems. In still other families, parenting difficulties happen without affecting the marital relationship.

In-law problems. The intrusion of in-laws might complicate parenting problems. In one family that came to our clinic, the mother was having difficulty controlling her early adolescent son. As an adolescent, the mother, then a wild teen, had become pregnant.

She ran away, leaving her son to be raised for four years by the son's grandparents. When the teenage mother returned to Richmond, a young adult, the son continued to be close to his grandparents. The mother married and she and her new husband reared the son for two years, but the son obeyed neither his stepfather nor his mother.

After several weeks of counseling, the therapist discovered that the aging grandparents had written the son, but not their own daughter, into their will. Wealthy, they held out the possibility of including their daughter in their will—*if* she pleased them. Whenever she tried to discipline her unruly son, he called his grandparents, who promptly threatened their daughter that they would give their estate to charity if the daughter did not cease her "harsh" discipline of her son.

Effective counseling of the parents involved having them decide that their son's future was more important than obtaining a portion of the grandparents' estate. After that, the parents stood up to the grandparents and discipline was more effective.

Drugs or alcohol. The abuse of drugs or alcohol by one partner can complicate your treatment of problems in parenting. When a spouse abuses drugs or alcohol, the spouse is out of control at times, and the abusive instances tend to focus the attention of the family. Not only do failures in self-control make it difficult to parent consistently, they also provoke denial and anger in the partners and fear and disrespect in the children. The combination can kill any chance of resolving parenting problems in five sessions of pastoral counseling.

Physical abuse. Physical abuse is health threatening. Mental health professionals are required to report physical abuse of a child to insure the child's health and welfare. In your state, confession of such abuse may not legally need to be reported based on pastor-parishioner privileged communication, but the situation is serious and can become lethal. You have a responsibility to prevent harm to those in your care. Take reports of abuse seriously and insure that the abusive parent gets help. Generally, abuse will not stop without external pressure.

Peer overinvolvement. Early adolescents are usually involved in their peer groups. This is a normal part of growing up. Sometimes, though, the peer group can exert an unhealthy influence over the child. The child may hang out with peers who drink, take other health risks (such as smoking or engaging in risky sexual behavior), vandalize property, fight, steal, or do other antisocial acts. The child may also become involved in peer groups who value things other than those stressed by the parents. For example, the adolescent may become materialistic when the parents abhor materialism. Many adolescent problems arise because parents cannot discern how to deal with such behavior. They react too permissively or too harshly, in both cases driving the teen deeper into the peer subculture. You need to know the extent of the child's involvement in his or her peer group as well as how the parents are dealing with that involvement.

How Are You Dealing with the Problem Now and What Have You Tried?

To make effective recommendations to parents, you need to know what the parent has tried and what happened when it was tried. As you gather history, ask how the parents tried to deal with the problem. Assess both the child's and parents' responses to each attempted solution.

What Resources Do You Have to Help You Deal with This Difficulty?

I wouldn't start to build a building without knowing what materials I had to work with. Similarly, ask about the resources that the parent has. These resources obviously include your own prayer and support, but other resources include both personal and material resources.

Who can help? Are both parents involved in parenting? Sometimes both parents work, so neither is available. How competent is the person caring for the child after school? Most parents seek help for problems first from a close friend. Does the parent have close friends who are knowledgeable about parenting? Is there a member of the congregation who has special information that might help the parent? Are grandparents or in-laws available? Do you know a good lay counselor who might help the parents? Is a counselor who specializes in family problems available and affordable?

What informational resources are available? Are there books that the parent can read? Videotapes or audiotapes? Are seminars available?

Are financial resources available for purchasing material supports or counseling? Is the home environment adequate to handle the problem?

What Have You Done before When Things Were Going Better in the Family?

Many problems can be resolved by employing the skills that parents have already developed but have forgotten about because they have become problem-focused. Have parents recall better days. Not only does this promote hope by restoring the idea that things can be better, it also helps parents break away from their focus on the problem and may lead to a creative solution to their problem with minimal counseling from you.

What Could You Do to Recapture Any of Those Better Times?

If parents can recall better times, they often dismiss those times as being irrelevant for the present. Stuck in problem focus, they may resist solutions. Challenge them to think of at least three creative ways to adapt a past solution for present use. Dislodge them from defeatist thinking.

Where Do You See God in All This, and How Can You Let Him Be More Involved?

When you ask about God's involvement in the problem, you get people to think about the implications of the problem for their spiritual walk. Often bitterness is revealed. They may have turned to God repeatedly to solve the problem and feel that they have been abandoned or that God doesn't care. They may be furious at God for not solving the problem in the way they wanted it solved. They may be puzzled at God's role in their lives or confused about whether or to what extent he acts in daily life. Asking about God's involvement will provide a rough gauge of what efforts you must make to help them increase their faith.

Some people may never have considered that God could be interested or involved in daily living. Your question plants the idea and helps them see evidence of his work to solve their problems, which may draw them to him.

Summary

In Table 10–1, we have provided a summary of these ten questions, which we arranged in four groups. To aid your memory, we created an acrostic—**DARK**—because the problem often seems exceptionally dark for those who come to you, until Jesus shines his light on the problem.

D stands for "Describe the Duration and Distress," which summarize the first three questions.

A stands for "Affect Other Areas," which prompts you to ask about the relationship of the problem to parenting in general and to other parts of the family members' lives.

R stands for "Responses: Recapture Solutions." Find how the parent is dealing with the problem and might have successfully handled it in the past. Ask how those times might be recaptured.

K stands for the "Kingship of Jesus." Jesus is Lord. It is easy for parents to forget God and his redeeming, forgiving, saving work through Jesus. Throughout counseling, call attention to the Lord and help parents grow spiritually instead of merely helping them solve their parenting problem.

11

Engagement Stage: Counseling Style

The engagement stage is the core of counseling. In it, you use your relationship with the person seeking your help to empower that person to become a better disciple of Jesus Christ within his or her own home. You show the parent how to live by faith working through love and help him or her apply those discipleship principles to problems in parenting.

You are a coach, helping prepare the parenting team for the big game, motivating the team for excellent performance, helping the team hold their chins high after defeats and getting them back on the winning track, helping them attribute victory to its source—Jesus at work within their lives. As coach, you aren't a player. If you rush onto the field you are not doing your job. But as coach, you have a vital role: to offer a strategic perspective. The players are often too close to the play to see a strategy. They may lose track of the big picture because they focus on limited objectives, on tactics. The coach provides a strategy that they can use to direct their tactics.

Counseling sessions are like practices in which you help players drill and discuss plans for the game. When the parents leave the counseling session, though, they enter the game, and there they must score. It is between sessions that parents must apply faith working through love to their problems and build their own and their children's Christian characters.

Counseling during the Engagement Stage

Goals

Keep clearly in mind your main goal for counseling: to create stronger disciples of Jesus Christ through promoting faith working through love in the family and throughout the person's life. A secondary but important goal is to help the parent solve problems in parenting using faith working through love. Pursuing these two goals should yield three primary outcomes.

- The parent will become a stronger disciple of Christ.
- The parent will feel less distress and will better deal with the child's problems.
- The child will be a stronger disciple of Christ.

Achieving these outcomes will lead to better relationships within the family, and parents' and children's other relationships will probably also improve. Namely, the parent's relationship with a spouse (if any) should be expected to improve, as should the parent's relationships with his or her own parents, in-laws, and friends. (See Table 11–1 for a ready summary.)

Table 11–1
Goals in the Engagement Stage

Main Goal: Create better disciples of Jesus Christ through promoting faith working through love

Secondary Goal: Help the parent deal with the problem in parenting by applying the principle of faith working through love

Results

- The parent will become more knitted to Christ.
- The parent will feel less distress and better deal with the child's problem.
- The child will learn better to apply faith working through love and thus be a better disciple of Jesus Christ.
- The parent's other relationships (with the spouse, grandparents, friends) will be changed through the parent's application of the principles of faith working through love.

Your Personality

At its heart, counseling is fundamentally an encounter of personalities. Successful counseling that accomplishes its intended goals blends the parent's, yours, and the Lord's personalities. It is tempting, when you spot a flaw in the parent's character, to feel as if you are responsible for correcting that flaw. That isn't your calling. If a person's character is to be changed, the Holy Spirit will change it.

Research on counseling suggests that some counseling techniques are successful, but it is more important for you to be the person that God created you to be than to practice any particular style of counseling. You must discern how you can counsel by balancing who you are, your present counseling skills, and your willingness to learn other skills that will, after practice, fit your personality. That discernment is difficult, and can take years of counseling and reflecting on your experience.

Style of Counseling

Throughout the encounter stage your focus was aimed more at relationship building and assessment than at providing guidance and suggesting options for parents' actions. During the engagement stage, usually in the second session, your style will change. People want answers to their struggles, and they pressure you to provide those answers.

Of course, you should not withhold answers from a person in need, but how you provide guidance is crucial to helping most people benefit from your answers. Because most pastors preach as well as counsel, they are tempted to move preaching into the counseling room, which usually isn't well received. Instead, within your natural personality style, follow these guidelines for directing your counseling style:

FEELINGS

- Take the parent's problems and struggles seriously.
- Acknowledge the parent's feelings first.
- Be gentle. Treat the parent as someone you love and respect regardless of the decisions he or she will eventually make. Acceptance is an important attitude for you to convey because many people expect pastors to adhere to a rigidly spiritual way of solving problems.
- Respond briefly but often. In the first session (encounter stage), the parent usually does more than half of the talking as you listen actively. In the engagement stage, the talk time is usually equally distributed between the parent and pastor. This shared responsibility for talking will help the parent feel that you value him or her and that you are helping solve the problem (but not overinvolved to the extent that you are taking responsibility from the parent).

THOUGHTS

- Ask what the parent thinks about solving the problem. Does he or she think the approach you suggested will work? Does he or she believe *any* solution is possible? How does he or she react to what you say?

ACTIONS

- Work collaboratively with the parent to form an action plan that will allow the parent to act differently outside of coun seling.

Content of Counseling

Holding your primary goal (to make disciples) and secondary goal (to help solve the problem) clearly in mind, spend most of counseling discussing specifics of the parent's problem. You need to know: (1) how children typically behave at various ages (based on a wider sample than your observations of your own children), (2) signs and symptoms, effective treatments, and qualified professional helpers for common childhood problems, and (3) your limitations (so you can recognize when you are out of your depth).

Using AGAPE

Throughout counseling, you will use the five-step method of AGAPE (see Chapter 5)—Assessing, Goal Planning, Acting, Persevering, and Evaluating—to deal with problems as they arise. AGAPE is a summary of the entire method of counseling, and it is a summary of how parents learn to analyze their own problems during counseling. Ideally, they can learn to apply the AGAPE method long after counseling has ended.

Summary

Instead of a tactical approach of telling you exactly how to diagnose and treat each child's problems, we are suggesting a strategic approach to helping parents. In the following chapters on the engagement stage of counseling, we provide a perspective on dealing with the parents' past and a summary of interventions that you can make to promote faith working through love in helping solve problems that parents have with their children.

12

Engagement Stage: Dealing with the Past

Parents don't come to counseling with an unprogrammed past. To the contrary, their history has provided a wealth of experiences on which they draw—consciously and unconsciously. Having grown up as a child within a household, they naturally think of parents in ways that are based on their own experiences. Those thoughts influence their parenting, causing problems in some areas and providing a positive vision for good parenting in other areas. Counseling addresses the past briefly to provide healing that permits parents to succeed in the present.

Understanding Memory

What Do You Remember about Your Past?

As you think about your own parents, what do you remember? You probably don't remember each day-to-day experience with your mother and father. You probably remember key events—traumatic or emotional experiences, epiphanies, and a "story" about how your parents treated you and vice versa.

Traumatic or Emotional Experiences

All adults recall traumatic or emotional childhood experiences. Emotional experiences are easy to recall because emotion stimulated glucose production in the brain, which helps memories consolidate fast. Further, similar emotional states cue our memory for the previous event, even though the current experience may have little in common with the previous event.

For many people, these memorable experiences occurred in adolescence because adolescence is a time of high change, a broadening social world that provides many opportunities for emotional experiences, and well-developed logical reasoning abilities that predispose adolescents to think about the traumas more than when they were younger. But many adults remember many emotional experiences that happened throughout life.

While we may think our memories of these emotional experiences are accurate, they probably aren't. Studies of long-term memories have generally shown that long-term memories are accurate in general but not in the details. My own mind rebels against that finding. I can remember some events in my life so vividly I would swear that they are accurate. But studies have shown that our memories are molded, shaped, and distorted by many things. For example, people's memories may change according to how they are asked what they remember. People who were asked how "frequently" they had headaches reported three times as many headaches as those who were asked how "occasionally" they had headaches. People who saw a movie and were asked, "How long was the movie?" answered, on the average, 130 minutes, but people who were asked, "How short was the movie?" answered, on the average, 100 minutes (Harris 1973).

People's recall can also be influenced by emotional state at the time of recall (Ucros 1989). For example, people who are depressed recall their parents as having been guilt-producing, rejecting, and punitive, but people who were previously depressed but weren't depressed when asked about their parents described their parents similarly to people who had never been depressed (Lewinsohn & Rosenbaum 1987).

Once we have an emotional experience, we *think* about it and recall, not just the mood or visual image, but also the words we used to describe the event to ourselves. As we tell and retell the story, to ourselves and to others, we embellish or impoverish the story. Before long, our memory of the event is changed through retelling. Changes happen gradually. A word of description changes, and the mind—which loves consistency and hates inconsistency in our memories—adjusts the visual image of the event. Then the remembered mood shifts. Further retelling of the story shifts the memory again. Over time, memories evolve away from the original event, though we are always sure that the event occurred *exactly* like we remember it.

Epiphanies

Epiphanies are sudden revelations, discoveries, or new insights. Created in God's image, humans are rational meaning-makers, who continually try to make sense out of their experiences. As we reflect on our experiences we sometimes get startling insights. Those epiphanies are stamped into our memories in the same ways that other emotional experiences are. The difference is that epiphanies are verbal understandings rather than events, but once understandings become memories, they become distorted just like other long-term memories.

Our Story

Each of us describes our history to ourselves and to others. That story helps us remember what seems important and forget what doesn't seem important. Our story orders the important events in our lives, creates a narrative, and illustrates it with memories that support the story. The story becomes an intertwined mesh of memories and connections. Forgetting occurs generally because we can't retrieve a memory.

Think of memories as food stored within a spider's web of associations. If one strand of the web is plucked, nearby areas jiggle and the food (memory) might vibrate. As we have new experiences we create new memories that we try to string together into a coherent narrative. As we understand our experiences differently, we build associations farther from the original memories. The strands leading to some memories may break through disuse until only one or two strands still connect to old memories that don't fit our current story. Some memories are isolated—forgotten.

Are Changeable Memories Good or Bad?

The changeability of memory can be either good or bad for us. If we dwell on the negative in our past, fuel it with new support, and never allow a positive memory to form without explaining it away as a temporary aberration from the normal, then our memories, visual pictures, epiphanies, and stories will become increasingly negative. However, if we infuse negative memories with faith, love, and hope, we build a web that is strongly tied to God and his sovereign work in our lives.

Most people think of themselves as passively remembering what happened to them. As we hope you can see from psychological research on memory, this isn't true. People actively shape, mold, and reconfigure memories. They thus can change their memories, but they need to be made aware of this capability so they can choose to positively affect their memories.

For example, Sharon has experienced many negative events in her life. As new negative events occur, she constructs a narrative to explain the experiences that say God doesn't exist, or if he does, he is cruel. She stops attending church, reading the Bible, and associating with Christian friends who make her feel guilty about her rejection of Christianity. By choosing a negative narrative, Sharon cuts off the positive memories of her conversion, times of joy in the Lord, and experiences of support and fellowship with Christians. After a while, those memories fade, and she now describes her life as one in which religion never played a part, or (if it did), she was deluded or brainwashed by pressure from her parents. While God keeps reaching out to Sharon, her memory prevents her from hearing him.

On the other hand, Martha, a woman with similarly negative events, remains in fellowship with Jesus and with those in her community of faith. She cannot help but encounter the work of the living God within the community if she but looks for it. As she draws close to God (Heb. 10:22–25), he draws near to her (James 4:8) and fills her with faith, hope, and love because he rewards those who diligently seek him (Heb. 11:6). She'll have new memories to weave into her narrative of faith if she remains faithful. God wants to help both women, but Sharon rejects his help while Martha receives it.

Healing

As a pastor, you are one of God's agents in the healing of memories. You help people create faithful narratives, not by making up things that aren't true, not by fabricating faith, but by helping them see what is true. Help them see God's acts of trustworthiness. Help them not isolate experiences of faith in their pasts. Help them create a narrative that accounts for negative experiences without rejecting a loving God.

Much of your work in healing memories will occur bit by bit as you talk and pray with the person seeking your help. However, you may also help more directly. A parent may identify a troubling memory as hampering his or her parenting. Pray with and for the person. The Lord can enter a person's memories and transform them in miraculous ways through prayer. The person might change his or her memories through developing a new perspective, relinquishing the emotional distress, or forgiving the parent for past hurts. God works wonderful healing of memories.

Prepare the Person for God's Healing

Help the person seek God, not healing. Only God can meet our deepest needs. He knows us, and he cares for those whom he loves. Preparatory conversation and prayer should stress the parent's need to draw closer to God through Jesus. If healing is the means by which that can best happen, help the person to accept healing in that spirit. If healing would not help the person's relationship with God (or would even hurt it), then help the person accept God's will in his or her life.

Help the Person Receive God's Healing

Have the person recall a specific memory as vividly as possible. Pray that Jesus would enter into that memory and transform it into a new memory. Some people will be able to "see" Jesus with their divine imagination and will tell you how Jesus resolves the past hurt. Others will benefit if you narrate an account of how Jesus might change the memory. Some may be distracted by narration. Spiritual discernment is the key to how you should facilitate healing of the memory. Remain sensitive to the Holy Spirit's leading.

Help the Person Apply God's Healing

When changes are made, they are often unseen, much like a bone that is healed beneath the skin. As with a newly healed broken bone, the person may be reluctant to place stress on the bone, which could lead to muscle atrophy. Healing a broken bone, though, requires having faith that the bone is healed and placing it under stress. Healing a broken memory similarly requires having faith that what the person experienced in prayer was real and valid. However, just as a person would not emerge from surgery and immediately play tennis, don't expect the parent to leave healing prayer assuming everything is healed. While the memory may be healed—especially if God has worked miraculously—restoration also may not be complete, and a period of consolidation and strengthening (like physical therapy after an operation) may be needed before full use will be restored.

Forgiveness

Part of healing past hurts occurs when the person who was hurt forgives those who hurt him or her. Forgiving is not forgetting. Just the opposite. Forgiving is acknowledging the other person's hurtful actions and empathizing with the other person. For example, if Frances had experienced defeat with her children because her parents had hurt her, she would need to forgive her parents. Help her understand how her parents could have hurt her. Yet, understanding her parent and even putting herself empathically in the position of the parent is not enough. Frances must renounce the claim to retribution, anger, and even justice and replace those motives with a desire for freedom from the past (for both herself and her parents). She might also develop a desire for the best for her own parents.

Forgiveness does not necessarily mean that reconciliation will occur. Reconciliation with someone who has grievously injured a person may not be possible. For example, a parent may have died, a divorce and remarriage may be finalized, or an abusive partner may be incarcerated. In none of those cases would reconciliation be called for or possible. Reconciliation depends on the offender confessing his or her sins to God (and probably to the person who was hurt) and trying to insure that such hurts won't recur.

Forgiveness can best occur if you help the person remember the injuries, confess his or her own parts (if any) in the injuries, empathize with the person inflicting the injury, relinquish retribution, and embrace forgiveness. You can lead the person through each step to promote forgiveness.

Summary

Counseling parents often leads into the parent's past. God has created memory as malleable, like hot metal, not cold steel. Memory can be changed. God can affect both a psychological and spiritual healing. Or bitterness can turn people's memories into misshapen grotesque caricatures of the past. Promote prayer and forgiveness and help parents forge memories that stand the test of time.

13

Engagement Stage: Interventions

Help parents address their child's problems by tailoring your interventions to the problem. In this chapter, we have described some interventions that promote faith, work, and love.

Promote Faith

Increase Family Spirituality

It is each parent's responsibility to nurture their children spiritually. God gives commands to parents in Deuteronomy 6:1–8.

> These are the commands, decrees and laws the LORD your God directed me to teach you to observe in the land that you are crossing the Jordan to possess, so that you, your children and their children after them may fear the LORD your God as long as you live by keeping all his decrees and commands that I give you, and so that you may enjoy long life. Hear, O Israel, and be careful to obey so that it may go well with you and that you may increase greatly in a land flowing with milk and honey, just as the LORD, the God of your fathers, promised you.

151

Hear, O Israel: The LORD our God, the LORD is one. Love the LORD your God with all your heart and with all your soul and with all your strength. These commands that I give you today are to be upon your hearts. Impress them upon your children. Talk about them when you sit at home and when you walk along the road, when you lie down and when you get up. Tie them as symbols on your hands and bind them on your foreheads. Write them on the doorframes of your houses and on your gates.

God directs all adults of Israel to love God with their whole being and to teach their children to do likewise. He says to structure their houses, their conversation, and their time to teach their children about God.

If either husband or wife assumes that the other is primarily in charge of the spiritual development of their children, that person is falling down on his or her God-given responsibilities. Therefore, at times, the husband will initiate activities that promote the children's spiritual development. At other times, the wife will initiate.

Help parents promote the spiritual development of young children through reading to them, telling Bible stories, and giving them a good grounding in the Bible. Encourage parents to help their children recognize God's power at work in the world whenever he acts sovereignly and to get to know God personally through prayer. Help parents teach children to develop the discipline of praying before meals and attending church.

Above all, parents *show* their children how Christians live. Children overhear adult conversations. If those conversations are concerned with how the adults apply the truths of Scripture into the parents' lives and the conversations take the truth of God's intervention in the world seriously, then the child can learn how to act like a committed Christian by actually observing committed Christians in action.

Parents help children grow spiritually by helping them deal with difficult questions, especially during the children's adolescence. Children should be allowed to discuss doubts freely. Their faith must mature from believing because parents said something was true to believing on their own. Parents should not fear their children's questions about the faith. Christianity has been discussed, debated, and defended by some of the greatest minds that ever existed. Christianity has answers. If parents cannot personally answer their children's doubts or questions, parents can help their children find answers from the multitude of sources available, such as Josh McDowell, C. S. Lewis, Paul Little, Rebecca Pippert, and others.

Promote Confession and Forgiveness

Regardless of the specific child-rearing problem that parents are dealing with, there will likely be a need for confession and repentance—both on the part of the parents and the child. Generally, parents don't become upset enough with their parenting troubles to seek help from a pastor unless they have experienced the full range of emotions (such as frustration, anger, fear, and worry), thoughts (such as doubts, self-condemnation, condemnation of the child, and perhaps criticism of the spouse and others), and actions (such as losing one's temper or withdrawing as a form of self-protection).

Parents will focus on the child's misbehavior and need for forgiveness and on their own unwillingness or inability to forgive the child, but parents will usually overlook their own need for repentance, confession, and forgiveness. While strongly supporting the parents, help them examine their own shortcomings and come contritely and humbly before the Lord.

Help the parents become better, not bitter. Their healing from sin will come through their self-examination, confession, and receipt of forgiveness. Throughout counseling, instead of allowing the parents to focus exclusively on what the child should do differently, focus their attention repeatedly on what they can and should do differently as parents to promote faith working through love. This is not to blame them for the child's problems. It is a matter of practicality. They can't change their child's behavior. They can only change their own parenting in ways that free the child to change. Help parents see where their efforts have not promoted faith, work, or love, but don't dwell on their failures. Help parents examine themselves before God without becoming a prosecuting attorney. As you well know, conviction is the Holy Spirit's job, not yours.

As parents discover their failures, pray for them and hear their confession on the spot. The world tells us that healing comes through blaming others or blaming forces outside of a person's control and by taking credit for whatever good that happens to a person. God says that healing comes through accepting failures, confessing them, repenting of them, receiving God's cleansing forgiveness, and through seeing God's hand working in all things. By helping a parent immediately confess a sinful action or thought, you promote God's view, not the world's.

Promote Work

Have Parents Identify Specific Goals

People who identify specific goals—and write them down—usually accomplish more than people whose goals are poorly understood and not written down (Locke & Latham 1990). To help dislodge parents from ineffective parenting, have them set goals *for themselves*. Most parents will say that their goal is to help their child get over the troublesome behavior. That is a worthy goal, but if left unadorned, it promotes inaction and blame.

Help parents express goals in terms of specific actions they want to take. For example, a mother might say that her goal is to help her five-year-old child obey more often. That goal alone won't be helpful. Instead, she should identify specific goals: (1) recognize and point out times when the child does obey, (2) give simple commands and short reasons (instead of long reasons, which have led the child to argue with the mother), (3) describe the consequences of disobedience whenever she gives the child a command, (4) have the child repeat what is expected and what the consequences for obedience and disobedience are, (5) don't assume that the child will carry out the command but watch the child to make sure that the child obeys, and (6) follow up immediately with consequences (praising obedience and punishing misbehavior). Further, the mother wants to (1) keep her temper under control when the child talks back, (2) explain clearly that the child is free to express her feelings respectfully but not disrespectfully, and (3) follow up immediately with praise or punishment. The mother will be more likely to accomplish those specific goals than the general goal of helping her child "obey more often."

Ask about the Homework

Each counseling session should provide the parent specific actions to do at home, for home is where the action is. Suggest that the parent write down any homework you suggest. Remember any homework. Some pastors record a note on their calendar at the time of the next scheduled appointment. Some keep notes in a file about each person they counsel. Some can remember without writing assignments down—but not many.

At the next session, ask (1) whether the parent did the homework, and (2) how it worked. Asking is crucial to having the person do future homework. If the person did not do the homework (or did only part), find out why not. Try to remove blocks that prevent doing homework.

Notice Successes

When a parent reports success at reaching specific goals—even small goals—always comment on the successes. Even during counseling, when a parent accomplishes a small goal, pay attention to it.

If you get into a "teaching" mindset in which you look for failures so you can teach better behavior, parents won't like it. After a while, many will resist your teaching. If you frequently point out a parent's successes, the parent will usually better accept your teaching.

Counseling is like our diet. Nutritionists tell us that we eat way too much fatty, cholesterol-filled meat. It tastes great but is unhealthy in large quantities. On the other hand, vegetables are almost always good for us, and few people eat enough. Teaching is meat—a little goes a long way. Recognition of successes is vegetables. It's hard to overdose on healthy vegetables. Serve a balanced diet to your counselees.

Reframe Failures Positively, as Something Parents Have Learned

When parents fail, they usually are discouraged. It's hard for them to see anything good from a failure. Help them see that a failure tells them what won't work. Don't spend much time on failures, though. Instead, get the parents thinking about what might work.

Promote Love

Help Improve Communication

Love is valuing each other, and one way to value another person is to treat the person as worthy of talking to. Regardless of the parenting problem, promote good communication between all involved.

It isn't enough simply to tell people that they should communicate better. It isn't even enough to tell them *how* to communicate better. To improve communication, do the following four things (not always in this order):

- Assess actual communication. Don't rely on how people say they communicate, which is usually different than is really the case.
- Make specific suggestions about how communication could be better. Then have people try out that way of communication.
- Draw general rules out of specific examples.
- Provide for much practice.

As you counsel parents to communicate better, apply these four guidelines. Get the two parents or one parent and child to talk to each other (at home or in your office). Help them to do the following:

- Express love for each other in words and actions.
- Share feelings in love. Help parents tell their children what they are feeling. Sometimes a parent fails to tell a child that the parent is "near the edge." Then when the child misbehaves, the parent "loses it," yelling, screaming, and berating the child. That loss of temper might have been avoided if the parent had expressed his or her feelings to the child.
- Listen to each other and show that they are listening. Some excellent books teach listening skills well (for example, Faber & Mazlish's *How To Talk So Kids Will Listen & Listen So Kids Will Talk* 1980; Gordon's *P. E. T.: Parent Effectiveness Training* 1975), though you may not agree with all that the books say.

- Pass information. Many misunderstandings occur because someone forgets to pass along information, assuming that the other person knows what is occurring.

Help Resolve Conflict

Three techniques can help parents and children resolve conflicts. First, teach parent (and child, if the child is old enough to understand) that what we intend to communicate is not always received as intended. When a parent detects a misunderstood comment, he or she can check out what the other person thought was intended. If there is a large difference the parent can clear up the misunderstanding and get back to resolving the difference.

Second, help parents see that more time should be spent in solving the problem than in defining the problem. In most conflicts, people spend 95 percent of their time arguing about what the problem is and only five percent trying to solve a problem. That priority is reversed from what is necessary to resolve differences effectively. Parent and child should state briefly what each thinks the problem is. If they can't agree on one problem, they should agree to try to solve both—one at a time. Then, they should concentrate their efforts on thinking up possible solutions. After they think of solutions, they can evaluate the solutions and decide on which is best.

Third, identify interests behind positions. Instead of staking out incompatible positions on an issue and locking horns, parent and child should identify why they took their position. They should identify the interests and needs behind their positions. The problem can often be resolved with both people able to meet all of their interests and needs—a truly win-win situation. (An excellent book describing this method is Fisher and Ury's (1981) *Getting To Yes: Negotiating Agreement Without Giving In.*)

Help Build Family Closeness

Many parenting problems erode the closeness between parents and children. Parents struggle to change their children, and children battle to resist the parents. Emotional closeness soon evaporates under the heat of discord. Help parents regain a sense of family closeness. Here are some ways that you might accomplish this.

Encourage having good times together. Families that laugh together become closer. Wuerffel, DeFrain, and Stinnett (1990) found that enjoyment of humor was related to family closeness. That doesn't mean that family members must do stand-up routines like Bill Cosby. Healthy uses of humor included, in order of frequency, family fun, quick wit, jokes, and other forms of humor. However, happy families did not use humor that put each other down.

Suggest doing what the children like sometimes. Usually, families do what the adults want to do. Katy Anna, our youngest, likes to play games and often asks for a family fun night, which translates into such games as "I Doubt It." Rarely is "I Doubt It" at the top of our adult agenda—as in "Hey, what'll we do tonight? I know. Why don't we invite the pastor over for a game of 'I Doubt It.'"—but periodically, we play because we value Katy Anna. (Once we get into it, it's fun, but we still don't think the pastor would thrive on it.)

Suggest having family adventures. Our family enjoys bushwhacking, playing hide-and-seek in the woods, backpacking, hiking, and car camping. We've had some great adventures. Like the summer we traveled to the Rockies, Mt. Rushmore, Yellowstone, the Grand Tetons, Bryce Canyon, the Grand Canyon, Canyon de Chelley, with stops to visit friends in Little Rock (no, not the Clintons) and Mississippi. All in four weeks. ("All right, we gotta make time. Nobody goes to the bathroom until Colorado.") We lost the alternator at the Grand Canyon, a couple of tires in Flagstaff, Arizona, the radiator in Little Rock, and various hoses here and there. That was the summer we bought a new car—one piece at a time. Looking back, it was, well, an adventure. Vacations provide an opportunity for family closeness by allowing the family to plan together and to enjoy breaks in the routine.

Show parents that teaching children can be fun. Help parents see that teaching should be done in fun rather than as a sense of duty or drudgery. They can create games to help children learn. We've provided some ideas in the companion book, *Value Your Children.*

Most people guide their lives in three ways: through the overall principles they adopt, the stories they tell themselves, and the images, songs, poems, and metaphors they employ. Much moral education has focused on identifying principles to live by. Recently, a greater appreciation of narratives has developed. The power of the image as a source of moral education has risen and fallen over the years, and we see good examples in C. S. Lewis, George MacDonald, and J. R. R. Tolkein, Frank Perretti, Robin Hardy, Steven Lawhead, Janette Oke, and others.

We can see all three approaches in the Bible. God taught through principles, such as the Ten Commandments, the Books of Law, Jesus' Sermon on the Mount, and the New Testament Epistles. He also taught through the story of his working in history—in Genesis and Exodus, the Judges, the Prophets, and the Gospels of Jesus' life, death, and resurrection. He also taught in images—for example, the Psalms, the Song of Solomon, and the Revelation.

Katy Anna has spent the year in both Sunday school and in Pioneer Girls memorizing moral principles. In Sunday school, the teacher held races to see who could find a Bible book first and offered donuts for all when every child had memorized the Ten Commandments. In Pioneer Girls, the leaders helped the children learn Bible verses by rewarding them with badges and praise. Instead of looking at memorizing as drudgery, Katy Anna sees it as performance.

At our home, moral education has been organized mostly around narrative approaches. We talk about the commandments when they are appropriate, but we have found great family enjoyment in stories. We read devotional stories, novels (like the Narnia series and Patricia St. John's books) from early ages. When we camp or hike (which is often), we tell progressive stories. I even wrote some Christian stories for the children. Since the VCR has come into our home, movies and videotapes have provided another source of moral stories. We don't merely get Christian videotapes. We also see old movies such as *Sergeant York, Keys to the Kingdom,* and *Joan of Arc.* We discuss other movies from a Christian perspective, providing an inoculation (of sorts) against influences of the world.

We have always sung as a family (except for Ev, who croaks and grunts) at home, on hikes, around the campfire, in the car. Singing is great moral education. In singing, people repeat the words, driving them deeper into their hearts.

Parents can promote Christian education in their children while still having fun. A book that is aimed at teaching values while promoting family fun is *Teaching Your Children Values* by Linda and Richard Eyre (1993).

Help parents support children's achievements. I was buying a soda in a fast food restaurant. I saw a couple talking to their two-year-old child. I winced as they constantly devalued their boy. "Don't do that. You never obey. You're an embarrassment. Bad boy." Children need praise for the good things they do, not a continual stream of correction.

Encourage parents to recognize their children's gifts and to tell the children and others about those gifts. Help parents learn to say, "God gave you an amazing mind. You're such a logical thinker," or "The Lord blessed you with great concentration," or "God made you a caring, loving boy." Over time, children whose gifts are recognized can accept and develop those gifts.

Many adults envy each other's gifts while we should glory in the diversity of gifts that God gives different people. It often is insecurity talking when we are jealous of someone else's gifts. Helping parents tell their children about the gifts they see in their children not only will help the children be more confident and secure, but it will also help the children eventually see the value of looking for gifts in others. Parents are modeling the virtue of recognizing the diversity of gifts God has provided to others.

Help parents give their children a forum for performing. Children love to perform: to sing, to dance, to put on a circus (turning somersaults and swinging on the back yard swing), to act in a living room play, or even to recite math facts. Help parents celebrate the child's sense of competence.

Through each of these guidelines, parents learn to promote love by valuing their children. Further, they model love for their children and thus teach their child also to value others. That is discipleship.

14

Disengagement Stage

In the disengagement stage, which occurs in the fifth and final session, help the parent solidify the gains made during counseling. If counseling has succeeded, the person should be a better disciple of Christ and should parent better. Also, help parents return to normal counseling-free life.

Solidify Gains Made in Counseling

Confession and Forgiveness

Help parents confess their sins, mistakes, and weaknesses rather than blame the child for all problems. Instead of creating guilt-ridden parents, confession leads to a Christian response—repentance and receipt of forgiveness and healing. In confession, repentance, and acceptance of forgiveness there is freedom to be a loving, God-honoring parent.

One parent I know berated herself continually for her son's every failure. If her son misbehaved in school, she should have trained him better. If he disrupted church, she was responsible. If he made a B on a test instead of an A, Mom was stupid. This Mom was like many others: a conscientious parent who was trained by her parents to perform to high standards and receive approval. She accepted responsibility for her son's failures, so she almost constantly felt guilty and inadequate.

Looking at her objectively, I could see that she was a hard-working, creative parent. Her son had great training, but he was human and had his own agenda, which didn't always agree with what his mother and father had trained him to do. Occasionally, he slipped out of his house after the family had gone to bed and roamed the neighborhood with a friend. He once went to school and sprayed shaving cream around the room of a teacher who had given him a B.

It took years for the mother to accept that her son was responsible for his decisions. At last, she could confess her legitimate failures in parenting without taking more responsibility than she should.

In the fourth session, ask the parent to list (prior to session five) ways that the parent might be blaming either himself or herself or the child for the problems. Say that during the final session you will go over the list with the parent and pray together for forgiveness where it is appropriate.

Parenting Using the Principle of Faith Working through Love

Throughout counseling the parent has applied the principle of faith working through love to a specific problem. The parent has repeatedly used the AGAPE sequence to discern specifically how to promote faith, work, and love. Review the main point of counseling with the parent—that parenting is (1) becoming a better disciple of Jesus, and (2) building his or her child into a stronger disciple of Jesus. Ask the parent to summarize what he or she learned about parenting. As the parent recounts his or her learning, ask the parent to describe how he or she has contributed to promoting faith working through love.

For example, Mary Rae (Chapters 3 and 6) has worked for five sessions with the assistant pastor, Pastor John, at her church. Mary Rae's daughter, Marita, was missing curfew, drinking, and acting disrespectfully to Mary Rae. Both Mary Rae and Marita had a negative view of their relationship, and both constantly criticized each other. Both were biding their time until Marita was old enough to move. Both were struggling with their faith.

By the fifth session, things were better. After the second session, Mary Rae had communicated better. In the three weeks between sessions two and three, Mary Rae had concentrated on listening to Marita and showing her that she cared. After session three, which concerned conflict negotiation, Mary Rae and Marita had a long talk about curfew, finally understanding each other's position on the matter. Employing Fisher and Ury's (1981) method, described in *Getting To Yes*, they agreed on later hours for Marita contingent on her calling to reassure Mary Rae that she was okay. They also discussed Marita's drinking, and Marita suggested that she wouldn't go out with the friends who drank, which would remove much of that temptation. In the fourth session, Pastor John and Mary Rae reviewed the conflict negotiations that had occurred between sessions and they role-played two other disagreements. During session five, as they prepared to disengage, Pastor John asked Mary Rae to re-examine what she had learned during the five sessions, which had been spread out over a twelve-week period.

Pastor: Have you thought about what has happened since we started counseling?

Mary Rae: It's like night and day—the difference between then and now.

Pastor: How is it different?

Mary Rae: Marita and I hardly argue now. We treat each other better. That's the biggest thing.

Pastor: So you'd say that you value each other more?

Mary Rae: Right. We don't devalue each other like we used to. We respect each other. I sometimes almost enjoy talking to her (laughs).

Pastor: You sound like you're surprised.

Mary Rae: I was making a joke. I know, I know (holds up hand). It's like put-down jokes that we talked about. I'm sorry. I know they're destructive, but I can't kick the habit. Anyway, I value Marita more. We've regained love by treating each other better.

Pastor: How did that come about?

Mary Rae: It started, I guess, when I began to ask her about her life and listen to her instead of trying to correct everything she said that didn't agree with my values.

Pastor:	That made a big difference.
Mary Rae:	It sure did. She felt like she was important to me, I suppose, and she responded better. She stopped being so belligerent and started telling me what was on her mind. Of course, it didn't happen overnight, but it did happen.
Pastor:	So faith working through love made a way through the conflict.
Mary Rae:	It sure did. I used to wonder, when you started talking about helping Marita be a better disciple and she wasn't even a Christian any longer. But I saw it work. She's come a long way in regaining her faith even though she hasn't recommitted her life to Jesus. She has come closer to being his disciple again, and she has learned more discipline.

Mary Rae and Pastor John discussed the counseling for another 30 minutes. They discussed three other ways that applying the principle of faith working through love had changed Marita's life. They talked about specific applications of the principle, which solidified Mary Rae's learning. Then Pastor John asked how counseling had affected Mary Rae.

Mary Rae:	I've learned a lot about being a better Mom. No, I guess I've learned more about being a better Christian, and one way that's shown up is making me a better parent.
Pastor:	That's valuable. How did counseling help you be a better Christian?
Mary Rae:	I look at the world differently now. Not a lot, but enough so that it makes a big difference. I look for more opportunities to value others. I'd have to admit, I'm a lot easier to live with and work with now.

Spiritual Growth

If you have succeeded at achieving the major goal of counseling (helping build the parent into a better disciple of Christ), the parent might report spiritual growth. Many parents, though, will become better disciples of Jesus, but they won't describe it as "spiritual." They equate spiritual growth with learning more about the Bible or praying more often, both of which are important. However, spiritual growth occurs anytime a person brings his or her life more in line with Jesus' leading by drawing closer to God and doing things God's way.

Consolidate spiritual growth by asking the parent to reflect on whether he or she has grown closer to God during counseling. Point out specific instances in which the parent has tried to align his or her will with the Lord's will. Tell the person when you see that he or she is living by trust in Jesus' saving work of redemption and resurrection. In pointing out these instances, you strengthen spiritual growth.

Help Parents Return to Normal Life

Assess the Parent

Strategic Pastoral Counseling is complete after five sessions, if not before. However, your relationship with the person usually won't end. Nonetheless, a transition is needed, and to make the right transition, you must assess the person again. The final assessment is informal, not like the more formal assessment when counseling began. The final assessment must consider the person's status spiritually, emotionally, mentally, and behaviorally as a parent. Armed with that knowledge, you can know whether

- to refer the parent to a mental health professional for continued and more intensive counseling,
- to connect the parent with a lay counselor for informal counseling, or
- to integrate the parent into normal congregational life.

Move Parents from Pastoral Counseling to Pastoral Care

Pastoral counseling is a labor-intensive part of pastoral care. Once counseling is complete, move to ongoing pastoral care. However, the parent may need additional help with problems—either because he or she has not learned to parent effectively or because the child has severe problems that need the attention of a professional helper.

Referral to a mental health professional. A mental health professional has more time to deal with problems than does a busy pastor. Further, if trained in family therapy or child psychology, the professional has special training in handling family and child problems.

Be aware of important differences in family and child psychology specialties so you can make an informed referral. Family therapists generally see children's problems as being within the family context. Usually, family-systems therapists believe that the family should always be treated together and they don't assign blame for the problem to any individual—parent or child. They assume that if family interactions are changed, the child's problem will disappear. Other family therapists may work with parents alone, child alone, or parents and child together. They may treat the child for a problem that they believe to be mostly the child's problem—such as (perhaps) autism—but also help the parents develop better ways to deal with the child's problem. Or they may treat the whole family together in problems such as constant disobedience. Child psychologists think of the problem as being the child's problem, and they might or might not involve the parents in treatment. In constant disobedience, for instance, a child psychologist might work with the child individually to learn self-control and compliance. The child therapist might (or might not) teach the parents how to discipline the child effectively, and in so doing see parents alone and then observe parents as they try to employ better parenting strategies. (See Racusin & Kaslow 1994 for a discussion of indications for each type of therapy.)

If possible, develop an extensive referral network. In rural areas and in small towns there may no therapist whom you trust. In those cases, evaluate the likelihood of harm at not referring the person versus referring the person to a non-Christian who may damage the person's values. Your best bet is to know the therapists to whom you refer.

Connect the parent with a good lay counselor. Christensen and Jacobson (1994) evaluated the effectiveness of lay counseling compared to professional counseling. They concluded that in most instances in which problems were of moderate or mild severity, the trained lay counselor's effectiveness was not different from the professional counselor's effectiveness. Only in severe pathology were professionals better.

If you assess the parent as having only moderate or mild problems, connect the person with a trained lay counselor in your congregation. Large congregations may have formal lay counseling programs in which carefully screened members of the congregation receive training in dealing with troubled people. In most congregations, though, regardless of size, there are natural helpers. Identify natural helpers and connect them with the parent. (You might recommend that the natural helpers read some books on lay helping. Ev has written some: Worthington 1982, 1985, 1994.)

Connect the parent to a discipleship group. If the parent has largely resolved his or her difficulties, integrate him or her into the normal congregational life. If discipleship groups are available they can continue the work you did with the parent in counseling, helping him or her to become a more faithful, working, loving disciple of Jesus.

Consider how the parent can best minister to others. People were created for relationship to God. Once in relationship, though, people were created for good works (Eph. 2:10). Help the parent put his or her gifts to use through ministering to others.

Encourage the parent to establish a memorial. With counseling complete, the person has traversed a difficult time in life, encountered trials to faith, work, and love, and emerged from counseling with a better sense of loving and serving the Lord. Like Joshua, who led the Israelites across the Jordan River into the promised land, the parent might want to establish a memorial to the Lord (Josh. 4:4–7).

The memorial can be anything that the parent uses to recall what the Lord has done. One parent might make a wall hanging. Another might create (with the child) a poster for the child's room or a laminated picture for the refrigerator. A parent of a child who struggled with academic work might frame the child's report card after a successful marking period.

Whatever memorial is used, it marks a transition from one side of the river to the other. It signifies that the journey in the wilderness is over and helps the family focus on taking the land. Taking the land wasn't easy for the Israelites, and it isn't easy for the family. Nonetheless, when the Israelites saw those stones that Joshua had piled up, they could give God the glory for his care and lovingkindness through the wilderness.

Summary

As counseling nears completion, disengagement necessitates the completion of two tasks. Solidify the gains the parent made through counseling. Then help the parent return to normal life. We have summarized your tasks during disengagement in Table 14–1.

Table 14–1
Tasks during the Disengagement Stage

Solidify Gains Made in Counseling
- Confession and Forgiveness
- Faith Working Through Love
- Spiritual Growth

Help Parents Return to Normal Life
- Assess the Parent
  - spiritually
  - emotionally
  - mentally
  - behaviorally as a parent
- Move Counselees from Pastoral Counseling to Pastoral Care
  - referral to a mental health professional
  - connect the parent with a good lay counselor
  - connect the parent to a discipleship group
  - consider how the parent can best minister to others
  - encourage the parent to establish a memorial

15

A Five-Session Plan

The theme of the movie trilogy, *Back to the Future,* starring Michael J. Fox, is the significance of choice. In each movie, the hero travels through time and acts heroically. No wars or social movements are started. No cataclysmic events occur. Yet one person changes the future.

The theme of the significance of human action in affecting human history is frequent in the cinema, as movies like Schwarzenegger's *Terminator* and *T–2,* Jimmy Stewart's *It's a Wonderful Life,* and books like Dickens' *A Christmas Carol* demonstrate. James Kennedy and Gerry Newcombe (1994) examine that theme in a book on history, literature, music, the arts, and culture, which asks *What If Jesus Had Never Been Born?,* in which Jesus' life was interpreted as the turning point of human history.

Great turning points often seem small at the time. They are momentous because they are *turning* points. A person changes direction and heads in a new direction. Counseling can be a turning point in a parent's life. The change might not look dramatic, but it could enormously affect the future.

Parents seek counsel for solving problems rearing their children. You can help them become better disciples of Christ (which is not exactly what they wanted) and solve their problems (which is what they wanted). Like the invalid who had been paralyzed for 38 years and simply wanted someone to help him into the Pool of Bethesda, but received Jesus' command to "Get up! Pick up your mat and walk" (see John 5:2–15), people often receive what they aren't looking for when they come to the Lord. But it is always what they need.

In counseling, don't expect many dramatic transformations. Expect turning points. Five sessions isn't much time for dramatic change, but it is time for people to reorient their lives when Jesus Christ is active.

In this present chapter we suggest a five-session outline for counseling. Use the companion book, *Value Your Children*, to supplement what the parent learns and practices in counseling.

Session One

Goal and Focus of the Session

Adopt three primary goals in the first session: join the parent in a working alliance, structure counseling so that expectations are clear, and assess the severity and duration of the problem in a way that will allow you to help the person practice faith working through love more fully. Encourage both parents to learn together.

Suggested Activities during the Session

Social phase. Act friendly and approachable, but don't create the expectation that counseling will simply be chatting about parenting. If you structure too quickly, you'll make counseling efficient but parents won't want to reveal their hearts to you. If you focus only on the personal, counseling can derail into socializing, making it difficult to accomplish anything that wouldn't happen by having lunch together.

The right balance differs with each parent you counsel. Many people who seek help from a pastor have never been to counseling before, and they have no idea of what goes on in counseling. Some may expect a sermon and a prayer; others, soothing platitudes; and others, private Bible study. Some people have experienced high-pressure conversion as children and they fear a reprise in counseling. Other people have no experience with Christianity, and they seek a pastor's help because they are coerced by a spouse or can't afford a professional mental health worker. Tailor counseling to each individual.

Transition from social phase to structuring. Greet the person and exchange small talk for no more than a couple of minutes. Get down to business by saying, "I would like for us to chat more, but if we're going to use our time together well, we should talk about why you want counseling. Before we start, though, let's understand what might happen in counseling." Refer to Chapter 10 (Encounter Stage) to refresh your memory about how to structure expectations for counseling.

Structuring. Say that the maximum number of sessions will be five, and tell the person that he or she will benefit most by participating actively in counseling. Describe the importance of making changes at home between sessions. Discuss the problem, and help the parent to see that her or his problem is to deal better with the child.

Assess the problem and its relationship to faith working through love. Discuss specifics of the problem. A focus on specifics is a key part of any type of counseling. Determine the duration, severity, and pervasiveness of the problem. Is it localized to one behavior with one child or does the problem show up with other children or adults?

As you let the person know that you understand the problem (by following, clarifying, paraphrasing, reflecting, and summarizing), observe aloud ways that the person employs (or doesn't employ) faith, work, and valuing love.

Ask the parent, "What, specifically, would you like to do differently as a parent when counseling is complete in five sessions?" This should start the parent thinking about his or her goals. Be specific. If the parent identifies exactly how he or she would know when success was achieved, then the person is more likely to be successful than if goals are vague.

State clearly, "In summary, you want to improve your parenting so you can help your child . . . (state specific problems that child has). More importantly, though, these problems have arisen because of weaknesses in faith, work, and love. For example, a weakness in faith was . . . (summarize one). A weakness in work was . . . (summarize one). A weakness in love was . . . (summarize one). If you can build your own faith, work, and love, and if you can help your child build his (or her) faith, work, and love, then I think you'll not only solve your parenting problem, but you'll do something more valuable— make yourself and your child better disciples of Jesus. Over the next four sessions, that's what we'll work on. How does that sound?"

Typical Tasks for the Parent to Accomplish at Home

First, assign the person to read Chapter 1 of the accompanying book, *Value Your Children.* Call special attention to the section on how to benefit from counseling with a pastor. Chapter 1 of that book takes the person through thirteen steps to prepare for change. Those steps are summarized in Table 15–1.

Table 15–1

Summary of the Thirteen Steps for Preparing the Parent to Benefit from Counseling, Listed in Chapter 1 of *Value Your Children*

1. Realize that you're not alone.
2. Admit your problems.
3. Examine yourself before God.
4. Examine your motivation.
5. Catch problems early.
6. Set realistic goals.
7. Be patient: Change takes time and hard work.
8. Change what you can.
9. Be willing to make mistakes.
10. Small changes make big differences.
11. Do what works.
12. Get a buddy.
13. Commit to pray daily for each child.

Second, the first session should sensitize the parent to exactly what is happening in his or her troublesome interactions with the child. Have the parent keep a log of the troubling interactions that occur in the time between sessions. The log should have three columns:

What Happened That Was Troubling	What Happened Just Before That Event	What Were My and My Child's Responses

Reviewing this log at the following session should help you and the parent understand specifically what the child is doing that is troublesome, what brings on the problem, and what happens after the problem.

Third, have the person jot down at least three things he or she would like to do differently as a parent by the end of counseling. Although earlier in the session you asked the parent about specific behaviors that would indicate success, you want the parent to ponder it between sessions and (importantly) *write* his or her goals.

Session Two

Goal and Focus of the Session

In general, the second session will be heavily concerned with history and causes of the problems. Focus on the parent's own parents (and the parent's spouse and his or her own parents). Your goal is to arrive at a clear understanding, collaboratively with the parent, that the cause of the problem involves weaknesses (in both child and parent) in faith working through love, probably with particular difficulty in either faith, work, or love. Use the occurrences in the parents' families of origin to bolster that understanding of the problem. Although you stated this clearly in session one, you'll find that few parents will remember it. Repetition is essential.

Typically, parents uncover some hurts from their family of origin that might interfere with their current parenting. A secondary goal, then, is to help heal those memories and help the parent forgive his or her own parents of those hurts.

Suggested Activities during the Session

Begin the session by asking how things went since the previous session, which shows your concern and allows you to discover intervening events that might affect counseling. For instance, a major car accident or death of a relative since the last session can affect counseling.

Discuss each item on the parent's log of troublesome behaviors. Identify instances in which the parent practiced faith, work, and love. Encourage success. Look together for instances in which the parent could have parented better by showing stronger faith, working more diligently, and valuing (and not devaluing) the child. Point out more instances of positive faith working through love than you do negative instances. Remind the parent that he or she can recognize where children have failed in faith working through love, and he or she can help children change by (1) modeling faith working through love, and (2) discussing issues with the children.

Ask the parent to describe his or her own upbringing. Be alert for patterns in the family of origin that mirror the patterns the parent is displaying in his or her current family. Those patterns come in two varieties—those copied or those that are the opposite of patterns in the family of origin. Copying parents is the most common, but sometimes people react in opposition to their parents. For instance, one woman who was sternly disciplined by spanking swore that she would never spank her child. She had responded to her parents' spanking by rebelling against authority, and she was determined that she would not drive her children to rebel. She was permissive, correcting gently and infrequently. Although her children did not rebel against authority, they acted with unruly belligerence toward authority, which they didn't respect. The result was the same.

Once patterns of weaknesses of faith working through love are uncovered in the current family and the parent's families of origin, enter into healing of memories (if that is appropriate). Review Chapter 11 for guidance about healing memories.

Summarize what you have observed—that the parent's specific problems (name some) are caused by weaknesses in faith working through love. Assign the parent to read Chapters 2 and 3 of *Value Your Children.*

Ask the parent what goals he or she wrote. Examine the list. If you don't hold the parent accountable for listing goals by asking for the list, the parent won't do future homework. After you examine the list, discuss and modify the goals with the parent and have the parent write revised goals.

Typical Tasks for the Parent to Accomplish at Home

First, assign the parent to read, prior to session three, Chapters 2 (The Cause of the Problem) and 3 (The Solution) in the accompanying book.

Second, have the parent continue to keep the log of troubling behavior, but have the parent add a fourth column: "How I Could Deal with the Problem in Faith Working through Love."

What Happened That Was Troubling Through Faith	What Happened Just Before That Event	What Were My and My Child's Responses	How I Could Deal with the Problem in Faith Working Through Love

Third, have the parent write some ways that he or she has successfully dealt with the problem in the past.

Session Three

Goal and Focus of the Session

The goal of the third session is to work with the major problem to arrive at a solution. Whereas the first two sessions were primarily focused on elaborating the problem as one of a weakness in faith, work, or love, the third session deals mostly with how the parent might increase in faith, work, and love to eliminate the problem and to grow as a disciple of Jesus.

Suggested Activities during the Session

Begin the session by asking how things have gone since the last session. Review the conceptualization of the problem. For example, say, "For the first two sessions, we talked about your inability to control Jerry and Jason's arguing and fighting. They fuss at the slightest provocation and you had about given up hope that anything could be done. We have looked at this problem as one of faith, work, and love. Mainly, Jerry and Jason devalue each other, and in your attempts to stop their fighting, you sometimes yell at and devalue each of them. Also, your loss of confidence that any solution is possible represents a weakness in your faith. You say that you trust God, but you have a hard time believing that he is able or willing to help with this problem. Finally, your discouragement has resulted in a loss of motivation and, at least before we started counseling, you were having a hard time working on the problem. Does that accurately summarize the situation?"

After the parent answers, either supporting or correcting your summary of the problem, state the goal of the third session. Say, "Today, we want to find several ways that you might be able to deal with this problem. We want to strengthen your faith that God can and will act in this situation. We also want to help you feel more motivated to work on the problem. Most of all, we want to help rebuild love in your family, so the boys will love and value each other more and you'll feel more like valuing them."

Review the parent's homework—to recall things that the parent has done that worked. (Look at what the parent wrote.) Discuss each item and find what the parent thinks might happen if the same idea were tried now. If the parent thinks that the old way won't work, ask why not. Help the parent think how the old idea might be modified to make it successful.

Arrive at several ideas that could be tried in the period between sessions three and four. Have the parent list those ideas on a "homework list." Copy the list for yourself.

Summarize how you have used AGAPE thus far—Assess, Goal Plan, Act, Persevere, and Evaluate. Describe the method as a good strategy to analyze problems. The parent will agree to the extent that he or she can see that it has worked in counseling. Have the client write:

A—Assess
G—Goal Plan
A—Act
P—Persevere
E—Evaluate

Many interventions, such as increasing family spirituality, improving communication, resolving conflict, and creating family closeness (see Chapter 12), can be employed during this session. Help the parent go beyond guessing at what might work by allowing the parent to role-play behaviors.

Review the parent's log of troubling events. The parent was supposed to write ways to apply faith working through love to the troubling events. If the parent couldn't think of solutions, help him or her do so in session. If the parent thought of good solutions, help him or her resolve to try those solutions at home. Add those intentions to the homework list.

End the session by asking the parent which ideas during the session he or she is most likely to attempt during the upcoming week. Encourage the parent to select at least three. The parent will be more likely to do homework to the extent he or she commits to try the solution. Assign reading and other homework and list each assignment on the homework list.

Typical Tasks for the Parent to Accomplish at Home

Between sessions three and four, have the person do four tasks.

- Have the parent read Chapter 4 (A Christian Vision of Parenting), which is filled with practical ideas about parenting and living as a disciple of Christ. Have the person add ideas that arise from his or her reading or thinking to the homework list.

- Have the parent continue to keep the log. Tell him or her to compare whether his or her parenting has begun to reflect the principle of faith working through love.

- Remind the parent that he or she has decided to try at least three of the new strategies between sessions.

- Have the parent list ways to prevent future parenting problems.

Session Four

Goal and Focus of the Session

The goal of the fourth session is to create strategies that might be used to prevent future problems and to allow the person to express the intention to carry out those strategies.

Suggested Activities during the Session

Ask how things have gone since the previous session. Review the conceptualization of the problem. Review the parent's log. Discuss whether he or she is more frequently acting in faith working through love. Praise specific successes. Ask whether the person tried three new ways of dealing with the problem since the last session. Praise successes.

Discuss specific instances in the log. Have the parent describe what happened, why strategies worked or didn't work. Depending on the parent's success, ask the parent to select new strategies to try in the upcoming week, or have the person try the same strategies again.

Have the parent show you his or her list of suggestions for preventing future problems. Discuss each in detail. It is common for this to be a short list. Help the person think of other ways to prevent problems using the principles of faith working through love. Assign homework to be done between sessions four and five.

Discuss a typical problem that still bothers the parent using interventions from Chapter 12 and approaching the problem using the AGAPE method.

Typical Tasks for the Parent to Accomplish at Home

First, have the parent read Chapter 5 of the accompanying book. The whole chapter, which deals with several problems, will provide information that might help the parent avoid those problems and will review applications of faith-working-through-love thinking, which will help the person use the principles. The chapter also allows the parent to think through the AGAPE method by seeing it applied repeatedly throughout the chapter.

Second, have the parent continue to keep his or her log. Ask the person to reflect on his or her current status. Does he or she need counseling from a mental health professional? Does he or she have a good support network? If not, are there people with whom a relationship could be established? How could he or she be more involved in congregational life?

The final session will in part deal with forgiveness. So, third, ask the person to list ways that he or she might be blaming himself or herself or the child for the problems. Those will be discussed in the final session.

Fourth, have the person list important lessons learned from counseling.

Session Five

Goal and Focus of the Session

The main goal of session five is to terminate counseling and return to normal pastoral care. Secondary goals are to solidify forgiveness, review the discipleship principle and its application to other problems, and to help the parent consolidate positive memories of counseling through creating a personal memorial to God for the work he has done.

Suggested Activities during the Session

Ask the parent how things have gone since the previous session. Review counseling to date, giving a brief summary of the focus of each session. Review the parent's log and discuss how he or she has applied faith working through love since the previous session. Such review helps the parent practice discipleship thinking.

The parent was asked to reflect on whether he or she needs counseling from a mental health professional, has a good support network for dealing with the problems, and has a good overall support network within the congregation. After discussion, recommend either more counseling, involvement in lay counseling, or full integration into the congregation—perhaps with opportunities to minister to others with similar problems.

Ask to see the person's list of ways that he or she might be blaming himself or herself or the child for the problems. Help the person forgive himself or herself or the child for perceived hurts. Examine the person's list of important lessons learned from counseling and discuss those lessons. Finally, if counseling was successful, describe the "Joshua memorial" and see if the parent wants to create a memorial, and if so, what kind.

Typical Tasks for the Parent to Accomplish at Home

After the final session, follow through with decisions that were made in the final session, such as (1) contacting a mental health professional, lay counselor, or supportive friend, (2) becoming more involved in ministry to others and in normal congregational life (including discipleship groups, if available), and (3) creating a Joshua memorial.

Summary

Five brief sessions plus work by the parent at home cannot completely solve stubborn or severe problems. To think that they could is unrealistic. Yet, the person can swerve in the right direction, aiming him or her, with more faith, work, and love, toward his or her heavenly Father.

Part **4**

Examples

16

Applications
to Five Parenting Problems

H ow does Strategic Pastoral Counseling look in practice? In this chapter, we illustrate how to counsel parents who are dealing with five different problems that occur at different points in the life cycle, and we describe how to conduct each session of counseling. We summarize each problem and how the case has developed, and we preview what to look for. After we excerpt from the session, we analyze the excerpt.

Case One: A Noncompliant Preschool Boy (Session One)

Background

Four-year-old Freddy was spoiled. The pastor, Sunday school teachers, church nursery workers, baby-sitters, and friends of Jane and Rob agreed. Now, after five weeks, so did day-care workers at Tots Learning Center—TLC.

After Rob had been laid off for three months, he landed a job as a bookkeeper. His wages were low, so Jane returned to work. In her second week of employment, TLC called about Freddy. When he was dropped off at TLC, he cried loudly and clung to the departing parent. Sometimes, Jane and Rob cuddled him and later slipped away, which usually worked but made them late for work. Sometimes they reassured Freddy, but whenever they tried to leave he threw a tantrum. Other times, they left in midtantrum.

At TLC, Freddy disrupted routine, refused to return games to their shelves, sulked when asked to do anything, played aggressively, and demanded constant attention from the teachers, who complained. At first Jane and Rob ignored and explained away the complaints, blaming uncaring and harsh teachers. After five weeks the teachers offered an ultimatum. Either Rob and Jane control Freddy or Freddy would no longer be welcome at TLC. Outraged, Jane called her closest friend, Helen. Helen listened sympathetically, but before the conversation was complete, Helen, who happened to be Freddy's Sunday school teacher, told Jane that indeed Freddy behaved poorly in Sunday school and in the church nursery, too. Helen recommended that Jane and Rob seek help from their pastor.

Preview

In the following excerpts, the pastor demonstrates two crucial parts of the first session. In the first excerpt, the pastor helps Rob and Jane describe the problem in specific rather than in general terms. In the second excerpt, the pastor assigns Jane and Rob homework.

Excerpts from Session One

Describing specific instances of the problem.

Pastor:	Tell me about the problem you're having with Freddy.
Jane:	People say he doesn't mind. They say he demands too much time and disrupts the school.
Pastor:	"People" say these things? Who specifically?
Jane:	The teachers at TLC.
Rob:	And Sunday school teachers. And baby-sitters.
Pastor:	And you don't think Freddy behaves like they say?
Jane:	Not really. He's independent, and very loving. He needs affection, and Rob and I have always given him a lot. I see

how teachers might not have time to give Freddy the love
he needs.

Pastor: So you see some basis for their complaints, but you don't
believe it's a problem.

Rob: Well, they insist that Freddy change or they'll kick him out
of TLC. Yeah, it's a problem.

Pastor: It would help me if you could describe one time that they
interpreted as a problem, even if you didn't agree.

Jane: Let's see. Humm. Last Wednesday, I took Freddy to TLC, and
I was early because I had been having trouble getting away
without him crying. So I wanted to ease him into school
and not cause me to be late. Anyway, when we got there,
he started crying at the door, holding onto my leg, and
screaming.

Pastor: What did you do then?

Jane: I told him not to worry, that I would stay for a while.

Pastor: And he did what?

Jane: That calmed him. He needs reassurance. He quieted down.
Then we went in, and two other boys were there earlier
than we were, so Freddy ran over and started playing. He's
a very social boy. Anyway, a screaming match soon broke
out, and one boy got hurt.

Pastor: How did that happen?

Jane: I wasn't watching closely, but I think that the boys had some
plastic armor and Freddy wanted them to share. They didn't
want to share, so I think he pushed one of them.

Pastor: Freddy wanted the armor but the other boys didn't want
to give it to him, so he tried to take it and pushed one of
the boys.

Jane: Right. He didn't mean to hurt the boy. He just wanted the
boys to share. Anyway, Mrs. Gomez rushed over to help the
boy who was crying. Then she took the armor from Freddy
and told him that he should *ask* if he wanted to play, not
push someone. When she took the armor, of course, Freddy
began to cry, so I comforted him. Mrs. Gomez said that I
ought to let him cry, but that's so cruel. It took a long time
to calm him, and when I did, he wouldn't let me go to work
without crying again. I was thirty minutes late.

Assigning homework. At the end of the first session, which lasted
an hour and fifteen minutes, their pastor assigned Rob and Jane a
task.

Pastor:	I'm looking forward to our next four counseling sessions. As I said earlier, though, we can't accomplish much during those actual sessions. *You'll* have to do the real work.
Jane:	I'm excited about making some changes.
Rob:	Yeah.
Pastor:	Today, we've described your problem as helping Freddy become less dependent on your and Rob's attention so he can get along better with other children and not antagonize the workers at TLC and his baby-sitters as often. You identified three goals: to have more faith in Freddy's ability to cope with problems himself, to work at not rushing to his aid immediately, and to value Freddy and help him mature.
Jane:	Right. I want what's best for Freddy. It may be hard for us, but I still want to try.
Rob:	I do, too.
Pastor:	Good. It would help if you both read a book about parenting called *Value Your Children.* You can buy it at *The Book Place* in the Tremont shopping center. Can you buy it this week?
Jane:	I think so. I'll get it on the way home.
Pastor:	Good. Read the first chapter before next week. Pay attention to the part about how to benefit from counseling.
Jane and Rob (together):	Okay.
Pastor:	Also, as you read the chapter, think specifically about what you would like to be different by the end of counseling. How would you know if counseling were successful? Make a list. Think of several things. How many would you like to list?
Jane:	I could think of at least five things immediately.
Pastor:	Good. Remember, list *specific* differences between what *you* are doing now and what you hope to do if counseling is successful.
Rob:	What about Freddy? Should we list what we want him to do?
Pastor:	List what *you* want to do differently. It would help if you could jot down a log of times when Freddy behaves in ways that you want to help him change. Keep this log during the entire time that we're counseling. You might want to purchase a notebook and bring it to each session. We'll examine those instances every week to plan how you can handle them better, and you can use what you've written to gauge your progress.

Jane:	Oh, I keep a notebook in my purse. I can use that.
Rob:	I'll use my pocket-size *Think* pad.
Pastor:	Good idea. Any time that Freddy acts in a way that you want to help him change, whichever of you is with him write what happened, then write what happened just before that occurred, and finally . . .
Jane:	Hold it. Let me write this directly in my notebook so I'll remember. Okay, what he did, what happened before he did it, and—what else?
Pastor:	What you did immediately afterwards—your response.
Jane:	Okay, my—I mean our—response.
Pastor:	So, summarize. What did you decide to do before next week?
Jane:	Get that book and read Chapter 1. Should we read the whole book?
Pastor:	You can if you want, but I'll ask you to read some of the book each week.
Rob:	I'll read Chapter 1. How about you, honey?
Jane:	I'll stick with the first chapter, too. Then we'll list five things we want to do differently by the time we complete counseling—things that we think would make counseling a success—and we'll make the log of Freddy's behavior and each keep a copy.

Analysis

Describing specific instances of the problem. At the beginning of her description of the problem, Jane felt defensive—accused by TLC workers and even her friend Helen. She presented a one-sided description of a time when Freddy misbehaved. In time, though, the pastor helped Jane describe the specifics more completely, giving a better picture of the problem than the general description that Jane began with.

Assigning homework. Whether people do what you suggest depends on how you make the suggestions. People will do homework more often if

- the assignment is clear and specific
- people understand how doing the assignment contributes to achieving their goals
- people repeat the assignment
- people say aloud that they will do the assignment

- people attribute the action to themselves rather than to following your orders
- you check later to see whether the assignment was done and use the results in counseling.

The pastor has employed each of these in assigning Jane and Rob tasks to accomplish at home, and they will probably carry out their tasks successfully. At the following session the pastor must ask about each part of the homework.

Resolution of the Case

Jane and Rob struggled throughout counseling. They never seemed to agree that Freddy's problem was as serious as others suggested it was, so their motivation to change was always low. Nonetheless, they tried to be firmer and to nurture Freddy in less permissive ways than they did prior to counseling, and Freddy became a bit less spoiled. Altogether this pastor's success at helping Jane and Rob was modest.

Case Two: A Third-Grade Boy
with School Problems (Session Two)

Background

In the third grade, Chris struggled. His elementary school used the third grade to introduce homework and tests into the children's schooling. After the supportive first three years, Chris did not adapt well. He refused to complete his homework and study for tests, and on his first marking period, he made two Fs, two Ds, and one C. He was distractable and often misbehaved. After he stuffed a classmate's jacket down the toilet, Chris's principal, teacher, and parents conferred about his academics and behavior. Chris's mother (Clarice) attended, but his father (Tim) had to work.

The principal had recommended that an educational psychologist evaluate Chris for attention deficit with hyperactivity disorder and for learning disabilities. She found no evidence of either. Disturbed about Chris's behavior, Clarice sought counseling from her pastor, Dr. Morrell.

Dr. Morrell insisted that both Clarice and Tim attend all five counseling sessions. In the first session, Tim and Clarice agreed with Dr. Morrell that Chris seemed unwilling to work. Dr. Morrell also noted that Tim seemed uninvolved in fatherhood.

Preview

In session two, Dr. Morrell had Tim and Clarice describe the histories of their families of origin. Clarice reported having an intact two-parent family with supportive but firm parents. Tim described a more turbulent past. The following excerpt involves Tim's account of his family history and Dr. Morrell's prayer for healing in Tim's memories.

Excerpts from Session Two

Tim: We had a dysfunctional home. My dad was an alcoholic and went on binges regularly. When he drank, everyone watched his step. We didn't want to make Dad angry. It was like walking on eggshells.

Pastor: So your father was around but often unavailable because he drank.

Tim: He wasn't even "around." When I was ten, he left home. No warning. He didn't come home one day. We were upset. Mom thought he'd probably gotten drunk and had an accident. She asked the police to look for him. They wouldn't look at first, but after a few days—when he still didn't show up—they treated him as a missing person. Never found him.

Pastor: That must have been scary for a ten-year-old boy.

Tim: I didn't know what to think. I don't think I was scared. I was sad but happy at the same time, and I felt guilty because I was happy. It wasn't okay to be happy if your Dad was missing.

Pastor: So you had jumbled up feelings.

Tim: I was messed up. Really messed up. For years. Even after we found out what happened to him.

Pastor: His leaving home disturbed you for a long time.

Tim: It *still* bothers me if I let it.

Pastor: I can see that it affects you.

Tim: It was worse, you know, finding that he hadn't been in an accident or anything like that. It was worse.

Pastor: Worse?

Tim: Yeah, worse. If he'd been, well, *unable* to come home it would have been bad, but it turned out he just didn't want to come home.

Pastor:	So he ran away?
Tim:	Uh-huh. Ran away with somebody he worked with. Moved to California. San Francisco.
Pastor:	And you were devastated that he could leave your mother and you for another woman.
Tim:	Worse. Another man. He'd been gay for years and none of us had the slightest suspicion. He'd get drunk in bars and go off with some guy. It was so, so cruel to Mom, to all of us.
Pastor:	To you.
Tim:	Yeah, to me.
Pastor:	And you've carried those hurts all these years.
Tim:	Yeah. I always wanted to be available for my son. I don't drink. I earn a good income. I'm faithful. I wasn't going to do to Chris what my dad did to me.
Pastor:	But now, when Chris is struggling with school, you're not around for him, always at work, overinvolved in activities. As Chris has developed more problems, you've become more distant. It's as if you're repeating what your father did, only different.
Tim:	I hadn't thought of it that way. I'm doing the same thing to Chris that my dad did to me, only different.
Pastor:	Tim, you seem to care deeply about Chris, and you don't want to repeat your father's abandonment—even though you are very different than he was in important ways. You seem, in some ways, bound to the hurts of the past.
Tim:	I feel bound to the past.
Pastor:	On your own, you'll never free yourself.
Tim:	I've tried. A thousand times. I can't.
Pastor:	Jesus can set you free from those bonds. He started his ministry by saying that he had come to set the captives free. Paul says in Galatians 5, "For freedom, Christ has set us free." John tells us that whomever the Son frees will be free indeed.
Tim:	But how?
Pastor:	He can work supernaturally to heal your memories through prayer.
Tim:	That's all? Just prayer? I've prayed, and I still feel bound.
Pastor:	You've prayed about it?
Tim:	Well, a few times.
Pastor:	Great. That's your answer to being free of the past. Maybe if we agreed in prayer . . .
Tim:	It might help.
Pastor:	Clarice, do you want to join in? Let's hold hands.
Clarice:	Sure. (Joins hands in a threesome.)

Pastor:	Tim, as you close your eyes, I want you to allow God to bring to your mind a specific time in your life that your Dad hurt you deeply. Are you picturing it? What's happening? Can you describe it?
Tim:	Yeah. Dad's drunk. Yelling. Then he just leaves. He's gone.
Pastor:	Lord, Jesus, we come before you, agreeing that you work supernaturally in Tim's life. So often he has felt the pain of a father who utterly abandoned him and the harm of finding that his father was gay. Lord, as Tim pictures his father in his mind's eye, we pray that you will minister healing to Tim's memories of his father. Tim, can you see Jesus entering the room where you are? (Tim nods.) What does he do?
Tim:	Puts his arms around me and says, "It's okay. I won't leave you." (Tim begins to cry.)
Pastor:	Lord, we pray that you'll fill with your Holy Spirit the void Tim feels from a father who abandoned him. You are his heavenly Father. Put your arms around Tim, please Lord, and free him from unforgiveness, bitterness, pain, anger, and hatred. Sever the ties to a painful past. Fill him with forgiveness and love for his father and help him be a better father to Chris and husband to Clarice. Show him his own shortcomings and empower him to rise, in your love, above those failings and sins. Help him become the new creation that you made him. Heal him, please, Lord.

As Dr. Morrell prayed, Tim, Clarice, and Dr. Morrell clung tightly to each other's hands, agreeing and uniting in prayer. It was a major turning point in counseling. As Tim became freer from the bitterness of past hurts, he could better help Chris.

Dr. Morrell saw what Tim could not see—that he was repeating the pattern started by his father, abandoning the family. Tim was distancing himself from his family through immersion in work and other activities. Chris, starved for his father's attention, sought attention through misbehavior at school, and Chris's misbehavior drove Tim farther from his family as Tim tried to avoid pain and disappointment. Until Dr. Morrell prayed with Tim and Clarice for healing of Tim's memories, the cycle seemed destined to repeat.

Analysis

Dr. Morrell did not rush to pray for healing of memories. Instead, the pastor first let Tim explore his memory and (importantly) his feelings about the meaning of that memory. As the meaning of his father's defection from the family became clearer to Tim, he could accept healing of painful memories.

Case Three: A Depressed Elementary School Girl (Session Three)

Background

DeeDee, 27 years old and a single mother who had become pregnant out of wedlock and had never married, became troubled over the unusual behavior of her 12-year-old fifth-grade daughter Tamara. Since DeeDee's own mother, with whom they had lived all of Tamara's life, had died, Tamara had acted differently than before the death. She was explosive, flying off the handle at the slightest provocation. All summer she had listened to her radio almost every day in her room, neglected her friends, and acted grouchy. She was usually eventempered and social, so the changed behavior during the summer was stark.

DeeDee called her pastor for advice. After ten minutes, Pastor Levan recognized that Tamara was depressed. He described the problem to DeeDee and told her that childhood depression often looked different than the sadness, crying, low energy, and apathy of adult depression. After getting a thorough summary of the severity of Tamara's symptoms, Pastor Levan concluded that her depression seemed relatively mild. He offered to work with DeeDee for five sessions to help her deal with Tamara's depression. Pastor Levan told DeeDee clearly, though, that if the problem became worse or if it did not remit within a month, DeeDee needed to take Tamara to a counselor.

In the first session, they discussed the depression as being partly due to feelings of helplessness, hopelessness, and powerlessness that accompanied the death of Tamara's grandmother. Those feelings eroded Tamara's desire to work. There was nothing she could do to bring her grandmother back, and she saw her unhappiness as extending interminably into the future. Tamara's faith was at low ebb. DeeDee couldn't seem to shake Tamara from her self-absorption regardless of what she tried to do, so she had stopped trying to help. Further, like Tamara, DeeDee's own faith was at low ebb. DeeDee became irritable and defensive at Pastor Levan's early attempts to find out what was wrong. Pastor Levan kept supporting and understanding until DeeDee softened and shared her heart. Pastor Levan and DeeDee then agreed to renew DeeDee's efforts to help Tamara and to trust Jesus to help.

In the second session, DeeDee discussed her past. In part, she blamed her mistakes on her early sexual involvement with the boy who got her pregnant. "Anyway, I haven't ever been sorry we didn't marry. He was no account, and Mama and people in the church have always been good to us. I don't want to see Tamara make a mistake like I did because she's feeling depressed." She prayed with Pastor Levan for God's forgiveness, that God would break the generational suffering that seemed to plague DeeDee's family by forgiving her of previous sins and freeing Tamara from their effects.

Preview

At the close of session two, Pastor Levan had asked DeeDee to read Chapters 2 and 3 of *Value Your Children*, which describe the cause and solution of problems. Between sessions, DeeDee called Pastor Levan and said that Tamara was getting worse, not better, so Pastor Levan asked DeeDee to bring Tamara with her for session three so he could assess her depression.

After talking with Tamara and DeeDee together for half an hour, he spent the last half of the session talking with DeeDee alone about how to handle Tamara's depression. We pick up the interview twenty minutes after it began, with Tamara still present. Pastor Levan had concluded that Tamara was quite depressed, and he had decided to recommend to DeeDee that she take Tamara to a counselor. This excerpt deals with making that recommendation and talking about how DeeDee might help her depressed daughter.

Excerpts from Session Three

Pastor: Tamara, your mother wants to help you feel better. How can she help?

Tamara: I don't know. Don't bug me so much, I guess.

Pastor: How does she bug you?

Tamara:	She comes into my room and asks how I'm doing all the time. I want to listen to tunes.
Pastor:	What can she do besides not coming into your room as much?
Tamara:	I don't know! I told you. I don't know. Stop bugging me. You don't understand. Adults never understand.
DeeDee:	Honey, don't talk to the preacher that way.
Tamara:	(Cries) I'm sorry. I didn't mean to yell. I just get so mad sometimes. I'm sorry.
Pastor:	I know it's frustrating, Tamara. You want to feel better, but nothing makes you feel better except listening to the radio.
Tamara:	Right.
Pastor:	I see that you're feeling sad and mad a lot. I wonder if you'd wait out in the sanctuary while I talk to your mama for a while?
Tamara:	Sure. (Leaves, looking over her shoulder as she exits.)
Pastor:	DeeDee, Tamara seems pretty depressed.
DeeDee:	She's showing teenage disrespect.
Pastor:	She might indeed be showing teenage disrespect, but most depressed kids are grouchy and irritable. She seems more depressed than rebellious, but I could be wrong. I think you should take her to a counselor.
DeeDee:	I don't know any counselors.
Pastor:	I know a couple who are good—a social worker and a licensed counselor. Both are Christians. I'll give you their phone numbers when we finish.
DeeDee:	Okay.
Pastor:	We have a lot to talk about. We need to discuss how you can provide more support to Tamara as she tries to get over this depression and how to give her more control and help with her self-esteem. Finally, you have to manage your own pressures. I know that having a depressed child puts extra pressure on you.
DeeDee:	It sure does. It's like a weight around my neck all the time.
Pastor:	I know.
DeeDee:	I don't know how to support Tamara. Everything I do "bugs" her, as she says.
Pastor:	I know it's hard. You think you're being supportive, but children don't always feel things the way you mean them. What has she responded well to in the past?
DeeDee:	Well, *not* asking her how's she's feeling. That's for sure.
Pastor:	What can you say to her that she feels is supportive?
DeeDee:	In her state of mind lately, nothing. Well, maybe telling her I love her. I haven't felt like doing that much since she's been so nasty tempered.

Pastor:	So she likes it when you say you love her. Great. How can you remind yourself to tell her that more often?

Analysis

DeeDee was discouraged and negative about Tamara's surly behavior, so DeeDee resisted Pastor Levan. Whatever Pastor Levan suggested, DeeDee either argued against or only reluctantly agreed with. Pastor Levan's challenge is with DeeDee, not with Tamara. He must help DeeDee develop effective strategies for dealing with Tamara by overcoming DeeDee's discouragement and negative frame of mind.

In this excerpt, Pastor Levan included Tamara in counseling. Although he had seen Tamara in a congregational setting, the brief interview with her helped Pastor Levan with more current information about her emotional state. He gave DeeDee a choice between two counselors, which is preferable to simply making a single recommendation (if two or more counselors are indeed available). He also helped DeeDee try to identify solutions. In the remainder of the interview, which was not described above, Pastor Levan helped DeeDee plan better ways to communicate with Tamara, and he briefly role played a conversation, showing her how to deal with Tamara's moodiness.

After the session was complete, DeeDee took Tamara to a counselor. In the final two sessions, Pastor Levan and DeeDee discussed additional ways that DeeDee could help Tamara benefit from the counsel she received and also developed some strategies for preventing misunderstandings between DeeDee and Tamara as Tamara moved into early adolescence.

Case Four: An Early-adolescent Girl Wanting More Independence (Session Four)

Background

Janet was thirteen, an early adolescent in full bloom. Her mother (Helen) and father (Stephen) weren't sure they were going to survive Janet's adolescence. They were amazed at the difference between Monica's (now seventeen) early adolescence, which went by like a dream, and Janet's. Janet was moody and argumentative, especially over her dress, music, hairstyle, and friends. Almost every word from her mother started another argument. "She's obnoxious," said Helen. "Either she's going to change, or I'll disown her."

Helen consulted Dan McGrath, her pastor, about how to deal with Janet's "obnoxious" behavior. In the first session Dan listened carefully. Janet seemed to be demanding freedom. Dan said that her arguments established distance between herself and her parents, and they also showed that her logical mind was developing. Helen agreed. She admitted that she didn't want to see her "baby" grow up. She also admitted that Janet's arguments sometimes rivaled a good lawyer's in their logic.

In the second session, Helen explored her memories of her own upbringing. As youngest of four children, Helen felt rejected when her mother went to work as a nurse when Helen was in the seventh grade. "She stayed home with my sister, but she kicked me from the nest as soon as I hit adolescence," she said bitterly. "She wanted to get on with her personal life." Dan and Helen talked for an hour before Helen could forgive her mother. Even in session three, she admitted that she was still a little bitter.

In session three, Helen and Dan worked for one and one-half hours on resolving conflicts between Helen and Janet. Dan taught Helen Fisher and Ury's (1981) method (see Chapter 13) of identifying the interests behind conflicting positions. They role played reenactments of two recent arguments between Helen and Janet—one in which Dan portrayed Helen and Helen portrayed her daughter, and the other with the roles reversed. They explored ways that Helen had diffused arguments with Janet's sister, and Dan asked Helen to try those strategies for three weeks between sessions. Now, after three weeks, Helen and Dan met for session four.

Preview

In the fourth session, Dan asked about any arguments. Helen described a loud argument over curfew that had occurred a week ago. Helen had sent Janet to bed at 9:30 only to awaken at 11:30 to the sound of Janet's radio. Helen grounded Janet for a week, and

Janet berated Helen for being harsh. Dan and Helen then discussed other ways that Helen could have handled the disobedience. Then Dan initiated the following discussion.

Excerpts from Session Four

Pastor: You have described a time when things didn't work out, and we've identified some ways to prevent similar disagreements in the future. How was the remainder of the three-week period? Could you see any successes as a result of the last session?

Helen: Sure. I didn't mention them because, well, I wanted to know how to handle the curfew problem if it came up again. But we had a peaceful week overall. Lots of the things I did kept disagreements to a minimum.

Pastor: For instance?

Helen: For instance, I tried to give Janet as much control as I could so she wouldn't have to misbehave to show that she was growing up.

Pastor: How did you do that?

Helen: Well, she wanted to have friends over. It was a day or two after our last session. Instead of organizing things, like I've done in the past, I told Janet that she was getting grown up and should decide herself what to do when Charlotte and Dawn came over. She said they were going to hang out and they didn't need any plans. Instead of arguing with her—I was proud of myself for not getting into a fuss—I said, "Okay," and I went on about my business. I saw her later that afternoon planning games. That night, she asked me if she could rent two videos for them to watch. I told her that was fine, and instead of saying that I'd help her pick them out, I said that *when* she picked out the videos I knew she'd make a mature selection so that Charlotte's mom and Dawn's parents wouldn't object and prevent them from sleeping over in the future. She said, "Fine." I'd have to say I was worried about her movie selection. Later, I saw the movies. They were silly teen-type comedies. I was so relieved.

Pastor: So you allowed her to exercise more control—within your comfort zone—and Janet did fine. Great. It's like we've said: you showed her that you valued and trusted her and she lived up to your faith. Faith working through love.

Helen: I didn't expect it. I really didn't.

Analysis

After counseling was complete, Helen continued to have periodic conflicts with Janet, but fewer than before. Helen realized that her bitterness toward her own mother for "abandoning" her seemed to fuel her need to hold onto Janet even though Janet wanted more distance. Helen confessed her bitterness and resentment to Dan and to God.

Case Five: An Aggressive Adolescent Boy (Session Five)

Background

Edward Whitaker was a case study in youth violence. He got in trouble for beating up two boys at school within a single semester, set an explosion in a phone booth (for which the juvenile court required 300 hours of community service to repay the damage), dropped out of school in his junior year, and finally was caught after breaking into a neighbor's house to steal electronic equipment. For that crime, Edward was sent to a youth correctional facility, where he served a year.

Edward's troubles profoundly affected his family. His mother was a high school teacher and a deacon in their small church, and his father was a computer technician and an elder. His parents felt judged and rejected by church members as the scandal unfolded. They changed to a large church, where they attended services and tried not to draw attention to themselves.

When Edward got in trouble with the law (public drunkenness) again, Mr. and Mrs. Whitaker set up an appointment with Dr. Springer to talk about their troubles dealing with their aggressive and troubled son. In four sessions with Dr. Springer, they concluded several things. First, Edward was responsible for making poor decisions that had landed him in trouble with the law, not they. Second, although they had made parenting mistakes (as do all parents at times), they couldn't undo the past. In the second session, they sought forgiveness from the Lord for their unintentional and intentional mistakes. Third, they had judged other Christians as much as they had been judged by the Christians. They confessed their sin and resolved to give up that judgment, with God's help. Fourth, they realized they should treat their son with love, even though they didn't approve of what he did.

Preview

They spent sessions three and four working with Dr. Springer on how to accept Edward as valuable without approving of his actions. In the fifth session (below), the Whitakers discuss reintegration into the congregation.

Excerpts from Session Five

Pastor:	You've made progress in dealing with your embarrassment over your son's bad decisions.
Mr. Whitaker:	We feel better. It'll help that Edward is joining the army. He plea bargained after the public drunkenness charge. He'll serve in the army and the prosecutor won't press charges. We've also shown Edward more valuing love. I think he needed that.
Mrs. Whitaker:	I'm worried about his being in the army because of all the alcohol used there. It isn't our decision, though, and I'm trying to trust God. In a way, I feel relieved Edward will be in the army.
Pastor:	So having him out of the home will make it easier for you to function normally again. I'm glad. I hope that you two will get involved in church again. For two years, you've essentially hidden from the shame of your son's poor behavior. I think you are ready to be involved again.
Mr. Whitaker:	You're right. We'll try to join a Bible study this fall.
Mrs. Whitaker:	And I might volunteer to teach one of the primary-junior classes in Sunday school.
Pastor:	I'm glad you're both more enthusiastic.
Mr. Whitaker:	I feel like we've been away and are coming home at last. God is good. I'd almost forgotten that. My faith had dipped lower than I had realized. I have hope now, for the first time in years.
Pastor:	I want you to consider something. Another family in the congregation is having difficulties. They're about your age. Their son just graduated from high school. He was picked

	up for drunk driving—his second offense—and the police found drugs. He's been court ordered into treatment for alcohol and drug abuse. With all the things you've been through, you might be able to help those parents deal with their troubles.
Mrs. Whitaker:	Who are they?
Pastor:	The Walkers—John and Val.
Mr. Whitaker:	I don't know them.
Mrs. Whitaker:	Me neither. What would you like us to do?
Pastor:	Nothing formally. Maybe call them and invite them over. I told them yesterday that I might ask someone to phone them. They said they would appreciate talking to someone. You are the perfect couple to help them.
Mr. Whitaker:	I'm not sure we have much to offer, but we'll try.

Analysis

Mr. and Mrs. Whitaker were eager to get re-involved in their new congregation, and Dr. Springer adroitly provided a way for them to help almost immediately while their excitement was high. He also provided a valuable resource for the Walkers. Now the Whitakers and Walkers can help each other be better disciples in dealing with similar difficulties.

Summary

Throughout this book we have stressed one central strategy. As Christians, our call is to help make ourselves and others better disciples of Jesus through following the pattern of faith working through love. Pastors have the privilege of passing that truth on to parents, who will train the next generation.

When parents have difficulties, those problems seem to the parents like emotional defeats. We can see them as doorways of opportunity.

Dorothy Gale, living a sad life in drab gray Kansas, was caught in a cyclone and tossed into the land of Oz. She moved cautiously to the door. Not knowing what she would find on the other side, she slowly creaked open the door. A world of color magically appeared. That new world was populated by dubious friends like scarecrows without brains, tin woodmen without hearts, and lions without courage. There were pleasant Munchkins, dangerous witches, and a humbug Wizard. Dorothy courageously entered the brilliant world filled with new opportunities and dangers.

Parents who seek your help are in much the same place as was Dorothy—needy, terrified of dangers, and yet courageously trusting that you, with God's power, will help set them more firmly on the true yellow brick road that leads to solving their problems in parenting, but more importantly to better fellowship with God. You have a road map that can help guide their way—God's plan of discipleship: faith working through love.

References

Ainsworth, M. D., Blehar, M., Waters, E., and Walls, S. 1978. *Patterns of attachment*. Hillsdale, N.J.: Lawrence Erlbaum.

Baumrind, D. 1967. Child-care practices anteceding three patterns of preschool behavior. *Genetic Psychology Monographs* 75:43–88.

———. 1971. Current patterns in parental authority. *Developmental Psychology Monograph* 4 (No. 1, Pt. 2).

Belsky, J. 1988. The "effects" of infant day care reconsidered. *Early Childhood Quarterly* 3:235–72.

Benner, D. G. 1992. *Strategic pastoral counseling: A short-term structured model*. Grand Rapids: Baker.

Berger, K. S. 1988. *The developing person through the life span*. New York: Worth.

Bettelheim, B. 1987. *A good enough parent*. New York: Knopf.

Bowlby, J. 1969. *Attachment*. New York: Basic.

Chang, P. 1994. Effects of interviewer questions and response type on compliance: An analogue study. *Journal of Counseling Psychology* 41: 4–82.

Cherlin, A. J., Furstenberg, F. F., Jr., Chase-Lansdale, P. L., Kierman, K. E., Robins, P. K., Morrison, D. R., and Teitler, J. O. 1991. Longitudinal studies of effects of divorce on children in Great Britain and the United States. *Science* 252:1386–89.

Christensen, A., and Jacobson, N. S. 1994. Who (or what) can do psychotherapy: The status and challenge of nonprofessional therapies. *Psychological Science* 5 (1):8–14.

Christenson, L. 1970. *The Christian family*. Minneapolis: Bethany.

Cummings, E. M., Davies, P. T., and Simpson, K. S. 1994. Marital conflict, gender, and children's appraisals and coping efficacy as mediators of child adjustment. *Journal of Family Psychology* 8:141–49.

deShazer, S. 1988. *Clues: Investigating solutions in brief therapy*. New York: Norton.

Dobson, J. C. 1970. *Dare to discipline*. Wheaton, Ill.: Tyndale House.

———. 1983. *Love must be tough: New hope for families in crisis*. Waco, Tex.: Word.

———. 1994. *The new dare to discipline*. Wheaton, Ill.: Tyndale House.

Eggebroten, A. 1987. Sparing the rod: Biblical discipline and parental discipleship. *The Other Side* (April): 6–33, 42.

Emery, R. 1988. *Marriage, divorce, and children's adjustment*. Beverly Hills: Sage.

Eyre, L., and Eyre, R. 1993. *Teaching your children values*. New York: Simon & Schuster.

Faber, A., and Mazlish, E. 1980. *How to talk so kids will listen & listen so kids will talk*. New York: Avon.

Family Research Council. 1992. *Free to be family: Helping mothers and fathers meet the needs of the next generation of American children: A special report from the Family Research Council*. Washington, D.C.: Family Research Council.

Fincham, F. D. 1994. Understanding the association between marital conflict and child adjustment: Overview. *Journal of Family Psychology* 8:123–27.

Fincham, F. D., Grych, J. H., and Osborne, L. N. 1994. Does marital conflict cause child maladjustment? Directions and challenges for longitudinal research. *Journal of Family Psychology* 8: 128–140.

Fisher, R., and Ury, W. 1981. *Getting to yes: Negotiating agreement without giving in*. New York: Penguin.

Forehand, R., Wells, K. C., McMahon, R. J., Griest, D., and Rogers, T. 1982. Maternal perceptions of maladjustment in clinic-referred children: An extension of earlier research. *Journal of Behavioral Assessment* 4:145–51.

Glenn, N. D. 1989. The social and cultural meaning of contemporary marriage. In S. B. Christensen (ed.), *The retreat from marriage*. Rockford, Ill.: The Rockford Institute, p. 118.

Gordon, T. 1975. *P. E. T., Parent Effectiveness Training: The tested new way to raise responsible children*. New York: New American Library.

Gothard, B. 1981. *Institute in basic youth conflicts.* Institute in Basic Youth Conflicts.

Gottman, J. M. 1993a. *What predicts divorce.* Hillsdale, N.J.: Lawrence Erlbaum.

———. 1993b. *Why marriages succeed or fail.* New York: Simon & Schuster.

———. 1994. Why marriages fail. *Family Therapy Networker* 18 (3):40–48.

Haley, J. 1987. *Problem-solving therapy,* 2d ed. San Francisco: Jossey-Bass.

Harris, R. J. 1973. Answering questions containing marked and unmarked adjectives and adverbs. *Journal of Experimental Psychology* 97:399–401.

Kennedy, D. J., and Newcombe, J. 1994. *What if Jesus had never been born?* Nashville: Thomas Nelson.

Kitzmann, K. M., and Emery, R. E. 1994. Child and family coping one year after mediated and litigated child custody disputes. *Journal of Family Psychology* 8:150–59.

Lee, C. 1991. Parenting as discipleship: A contextual motif for Christian parent education. *Journal of Psychology and Theology* 19: 268–277.

Lewinsohn, P. M., and Rosenbaum, M. 1987. Recall of parental behavior by acute depressives, remitted depressives, and nondepressives. *Journal of Personality and Social Psychology* 52:611–19.

Locke, E. A., and Latham, G. P. 1990. *A theory of goal setting and task performance.* Englewood Cliffs, N.J.: Prentice-Hall.

Miller, S., Wackman, D. B., Nunnally, E. W., and Miller, P. A. 1988. *Connecting: With self and others.* Littleton, Colo.: Interpersonal Communication Programs.

Montessori, M. 1964. *The Montessori method.* New York: Schocken Books.

———. 1972. *Education and peace* (trans. Helen R. Lane). Chicago: Henry Regnery Company.

Narramore, B. 1972. *Help! I'm a parent.* Grand Rapids, Mich.: Zondervan.

Nock, S. L., and Kingston, P. W. 1988. Time with children: The impact of couples' work-time commitments. *Social Forces* 67:59–85.

Olson, D. H., McCubbin, H. I., Barnes, H., Larsen, A., Muxen, M., and Wilson, M. 1983. *Families: What makes them work.* Beverly Hills: Sage.

Piaget, J. 1959. *The language and thought of the child,* 3d ed. (trans. Marjorie Gabain and Ruth Gabain). London: Routledge and Kegan Paul.

Porter, E. H. 1913. *Pollyanna.* New York: Grosset & Dunlap.

Prange, G. W., with Goldstein, D. M., and Dillon, K. V. 1990. *God's Samurai: Lead pilot at Pearl Harbor*. Washington, D.C.: Brassey's.

Racusin, G. R., and Kaslow, N. J. 1994. Child and family therapy combined: Indications and implications. *American Journal of Family Therapy* 22:237–46.

Robinson, J. P. 1977. *How Americans use their time: A social-psychological analysis of everyday behavior*. New York: Praeger.

————. 1989. Caring for kids. *American Demographics* July:52.

Rogers, C. R. 1951. *Client-centered therapy*. Boston: Houghton-Mifflin.

Rutter, M. 1994. Family discord and conduct disorder: Cause, consequence, or correlate? *Journal of Family Psychology* 8:170–86.

Seligman, M. E. P. 1991. *Learned optimism*. New York: Random House.

Sheldon, C. M. 1985. *In his steps*. Westwood, N.J.: Barbour.

Spock, B. 1945. *The common sense book of baby and child care*. New York: Duell, Sloan, and Pearce.

Strommen, M. P., and Strommen, A. I. 1985. *Five cries of parents: New help for families on the issues that trouble them most*. San Francisco: Harper & Row.

U. S. Bureau of the Census. Annual. *Current population reports*, series P–20. U. S. Bureau of the Census: Washington, D.C.

Ucros, C. G. 1989. Mood state-dependent memory: A meta-analysis. *Cognition and Emotion* 3:139–67.

Visher, E. B., and Visher, J. S. 1988. *Old loyalties, new ties: Therapeutic strategies with stepfamilies*. New York: Brunner/Mazel.

Wallerstein, J. S., and Blakeslee, S. 1990. *Second chances: Men, women, and children a decade after divorce*. New York: Ticknor & Fields.

Worthington, E. L., Jr. 1982. *When someone asks for help: A practical guide for counseling*. Downers Grove, Ill.: InterVarsity Press.

————. 1982. *How to help the hurting: When friends face problems with self-esteem, self-control, fear, depression, loneliness*. Downers Grove, Ill.: InterVarsity Press.

————. 1992. Family counseling: An approach that works. *Christian Counseling Today* Premier Issue: 13–17.

————. 1994. *I care about your marriage: Helping friends and families with marital problems*. Chicago: Moody.

Worthington, E. L., Jr., and McMurry, D. 1994. *Marriage conflicts*. Grand Rapids, Mich.: Baker.

Wuerffel, J., DeFrain, J., and Stinnett, N. 1990. How strong families use humor. *Family Perspective* 24:129–42.